Counseling People with Cancer

Counseling and Pastoral Theology

Andrew D. Lester, Series Editor

Counseling People
with Cancer

Jann Aldredge-Clanton

Westminster John Knox Press
Louisville, Kentucky

Book design by Jennifer K. Cox
Cover design by Kevin Darst

First edition
Published by Westminster John Knox Press
Louisville, Kentucky

This book is printed on acid-free paper that meets the
American National Standards Institute Z39.48 standard. ♾

PRINTED IN THE UNITED STATES OF AMERICA
98 99 00 01 02 03 04 05 06 07 — 10 9 8 7 6 5 4 3 2 1

Library of Congress Cataloging-in-Publication Data

Aldredge-Clanton, Jann, date.
    Counseling people with cancer / Jann Aldredge-Clanton. — 1st ed.
        p.   cm. — (Counseling and pastoral theology)
    Includes bibliographical references and index.
    ISBN 0-664-25666-X (alk. paper)
    1. Cancer—Patients—Pastoral counseling of. 2. Church work with
the sick. 3. Hope—Religious aspects—Christianity. I. Title.
II. Series.
BV4335.A44   1998
259'.4196994—dc21   97-28816

Contents

Foreword

Jann Aldredge-Clanton lost her father to cancer of the spine after a difficult nine-week struggle with this aggressive intruder. From that experience, and from her ministry as an oncology chaplain and a pastoral counselor, she has written this thoughtful, inspiring book on caring for people suffering with cancer. She wrote it as a gift to her father and to all those "who have profoundly influenced my life by the way they met the challenge of cancer."

Cancer strikes one out of three people in the United States and causes one out of four deaths. Few diseases evoke images of suffering, dehumanization, and death as does cancer—the modern "archetypal symbol of misfortune and death," as one writer put it (see chap. 1, n.2). The diagnosis of cancer, therefore, precipitates psychological and spiritual crises that accompany the physical problems. The diagnosis of cancer, and the suffering that often attends this disease process, can raise existential questions about meaning, purpose, and values. In this context, ministers have an opportunity to provide care and counseling that focus on central issues of faith and spirituality.

Despair is never far away from people suffering with cancer, and is frequently overwhelming. Hope, therefore, is the central theological theme of this book. The author agrees with Jürgen Moltmann's contention that hope is the most realistic of all human dynamics because hope takes seriously all the possibilities that lie in front of us. The concepts in this book help ministers develop creative ways of inviting people with cancer to experience hope.

Aldredge-Clanton knows the importance of allowing people with cancer to tell their unique stories. She uses narrative theology as a context for understanding the importance of sacred stories for better—or worse! Although some sacred stories are distressing and lead to despair, she describes the powerful potential of sacred stories that emphasize God's love and care to lead from despair to hope.

Unique in this book are some ideas about the significance of sacred images. A diagnosis of cancer challenges, and often changes, a person's understanding of God. When cancer raises "Why?" questions, the answers provided by a person's previous religious experience may not be adequate. Sacred images from the past must be reviewed and evaluated to find those that are life giving and hopeful. The minister can be a spiritual guide as people with cancer revalue, reexamine, and transform their sacred images and stories in ways that bring healing. These chapters are filled with stories of creative God-images that have enabled patients to develop new spiritual insight, overcome despair, and rejoice in a creative new hope.

Aldredge-Clanton explores many psychospiritual responses to the experience of cancer: depression, anxiety, anger, helplessness, grief, shame, loneliness, and loss of self-esteem. Since cancer challenges body images and sexual identity, one chapter deals with the issue of embodiment. Another chapter discusses the difficulty of deciding what treatments, if any, to undergo—an ethical dilemma.

In summary, this book is a comprehensive companion for those who offer pastoral care and counseling to people facing the diagnosis of cancer and the major changes in life brought about by the long process of treatment and the uncertain future that usually follows.

The Counseling and Pastoral Theology Series

The purpose of this series is to address clinical issues that arise among particular populations currently neglected in the literature on pastoral care and counseling (women in lesbian relationships, African American couples, adolescents under stress, women who are depressed, survivors of sexual abuse, adult adoptees, people with terminal illness, and couples experiencing infertility). This series is committed to enhancing both the theoretical base and the clinical expertise of pastoral caregivers by providing a pastoral theological paradigm that will inform both assessment and intervention with people in these specific populations.

Many books dealing with pastoral care and counseling are more carefully informed by the behavioral and social sciences than by classical theological disciplines. Pastoral care and counseling specialists have been criticized for ignoring our theological heritage and challenged to reevaluate our idolization of psychology and claim our unique perspectives on the human predicament. The discipline of pastoral theology has made significant strides in the past decade. The Society for Pastoral Theology was formed in 1985 and now publishes the *Journal of Pastoral Theology*.

Pastoral theology grows out of data gathered from at least three sources: (1) revelation about the human condition uncovered by the social and behavioral sciences, (2) wisdom from the classical theological disciplines, and (3) insight garnered from reflection on the pastoral ministry event. The development of pastoral theology grows out of the dialogue among these three perspectives, each perspective enabled to ask questions of, challenge, and critique the other perspectives.

Each author is clinically experienced and academically prepared to write about the particular population with which she or he is personally concerned and professionally involved. Each author develops a "constructive pastoral theology," developing the theological frame of reference that provides the unique perspective from which a pastoral person approaches both assessment and intervention. This constructive pastoral theology will enable clinically trained pastors and pastoral care specialists (pastoral counselors, chaplains, clinical pastoral education supervisors) to creatively participate in pastoral relationships that effectively enable healing, sustaining, guiding, reconciling, and liberating.

Though the focus will be on offering pastoral care and counseling to individuals, couples, and families, each author is cognizant of the interaction between individuals and their environment. These books will consider the effects of larger systems—from family of origin to cultural constructs. Each author will use case material from her or his clinical pastoral ministry which will serve to focus the reader's attention on the issues faced by the particular population as viewed from the pastoral theological paradigm.

My thanks to colleagues who faithfully served on the Advisory Committee and spent many hours in creative work to ensure that this series would make a substantial contribution: Bonnie Miller-McLemore (1992–96), Nancy Ramsay (1992–96), Han van den Blink (1992–94), Larry Graham (1994–96), Linda Kirkland-Harris (1994–96).

Andrew D. Lester
Brite Divinity School

Acknowledgments

My deepest gratitude goes to the people with cancer who generously and gladly contributed their experiences as clinical material for this book. I owe an enormous debt to these courageous and wise people who have opened my eyes to see more fully into ministry and into life in general. This is as much their book as mine, so integral are their stories to the book's content and spirit. Thank you, gracious people.

The general editor of this book and series on pastoral counseling, Andrew Lester, played an invaluable role in every stage of this book's generation. I am indeed grateful to Andy for inviting me to write the book and for being an insightful, encouraging partner throughout the creative process. His pastoral theology of hope influenced the conceptual foundation of this book. My thanks also to Jon Berquist, Stephanie Egnotovich, and Carl Helmich, my editors at Westminster John Knox, for their careful shepherding of the book to its final form.

My deep appreciation goes to Ann Johnson, Travis Maxwell, Katherine Norvell, and Nancy Ellett Allison for their generous gifts of time, energy, and expertise. Their perceptive, thorough critiques of my manuscript strengthened its content and style. I am also grateful for the support and encouragement of all my colleagues in the Department of Pastoral Care and Counseling at Baylor University Medical Center.

The loving support of my husband, David, was especially important to the completion of this project. It was often hard to come home from ministry with persons experiencing cancer and to find enough energy left to write about these experiences. I am deeply thankful to David for always being there to listen, to offer valuable suggestions about the book's content and style, and to give nurturing affirmation.

Introduction

Some thirty years ago I received a call from my mother asking me to come as quickly as possible to the hospital where my father had gone a few days earlier for a series of tests. I could tell by the trembling in her voice that something was wrong. My father, who at that time was pastor of a church in Minden, Louisiana, had been having back pain for several months. He had gone to several doctors who had assured him that the pain was from pulled muscles. Surely that's all it was, I tried to tell myself as I drove as fast as I could from Ruston, where I was a sophomore at Louisiana Polytechnic University, to the hospital in Shreveport. One look at my mother's face told me there was more. Through her sobs, she said that doctors had found an aggressive cancer in his spine. She made an effort to give me a more specific explanation of the diagnosis, which physicians at that time labeled "lymphosarcoma," with probable metastasis to the liver and bone. All I heard were the words "aggressive cancer," and my heart pounded up through my chest into my throat as questions exploded in my mind: How can this be? What about pulled muscles? Can there be some mistake? How can this be, when he's only fifty-four? Why would this happen to someone who had given his life to the ministry? Why would it happen to him when he was in the prime of his ministry? God, surely you wouldn't let this happen?

During the next nine weeks I watched my father suffer devastating losses and agonizing pain. He did not get to preach the Easter sermon he had so passionately prepared, nor any other sermon ever again. The spread of the cancer in his spinal column and into his brain caused paralysis from his waist down and then blindness. A brilliant man who had always loved to read, my father found the loss of his eyesight almost unbearable. Mercifully and miraculously, he regained his sight after a few weeks. His increasing pain, however, necessitated more and more medication so that he gradually lost his ability to concentrate on a book for any length of time. His physical, mental, and spiritual suffering reached the point that one day he cried out, like Job, that he wished he had never been born. He didn't know that I was standing outside the door and heard his agonized cry.

Through these painful nine weeks there were also times of joy and laughter and transcendence. The stories my mother, father, sister Anne, and I told, especially of family vacations, transported us beyond the hospital room. Relief came also through the humorous cards my father's brother sent every day. The church my father pastored surrounded us with constant love and attention, appointing members to be on call for us round the clock. These caring people brought food, drove my grandparents back and forth to the hospital, and sat praying in the hospital lobby, waiting to see if there was anything else they could do. Though I didn't realize it at the time, my image of God as Loving Community was developing.

One of my father's most earnest prayers was answered: that he not lose any mental functioning. His mind and spirit seemed to grow fuller and his voice to grow richer, even as his body deteriorated. The last week of his life, his imagination expanded into the future as he talked with us and with his nurses about his vision of heaven. His deep baritone singing of "There is a Balm in Gilead" filled the room and the entire hall with hope and beauty. The night he died he was alert until the last few minutes. Mother, Anne, and I stood around his bed as he told each one of us how much he loved us and then asked us to sing his favorite hymns. He died as we were singing "Amazing Grace."

Anne Lamott, in her book *Bird by Bird: Some Instructions on Writing and Life*, talks about writing books as presents to people.[1] As I am finishing this book, writing the introduction last, as I often do, I realize that I have written it as a gift to my father and to all the other people who have profoundly influenced my life by the way they met the challenge of cancer. These courageous people have given to me from the depths and heights of their experience as I have been in relationship with them, first as daughter with my father and then as friend with several people and then as minister with people in a local parish, in a counseling center, and in several medical centers. My gift to them is this effort to represent and interpret the cancer experience in ways that will deepen the understanding and improve the art of those who minister with people going through cancer.

Ministers of all kinds and in all settings are increasingly finding themselves in relationships with people experiencing cancer. One out of three persons in the United States will experience cancer in his or her lifetime.[2] One of every four deaths in the United States is from cancer.[3] Thus most congregations in this country have many members with cancer, and most families are touched by cancer. It is important, then, for seminarians and ministers to develop an understanding of the psychosocial and spiritual dynamics of people with cancer and to acquire the pastoral skills necessary to minister effectively.

Henri Nouwen has written that "perhaps the main task of the minister is to prevent people from suffering for the wrong reasons." He goes on to say that many people suffer because they have based their lives on the false supposition that there should be no fear, loneliness, confusion, or doubt— that is, that there should be no suffering. Ministers, then, are to guide people to understand that suffering is integral to the human condition so that they can deal creatively with suffering. When we realize "that we do not have to escape our pains, but that we can mobilize them into a common search for life, those very pains are transformed from expressions of despair into signs of hope."[4]

A major theological theme for this book is hope. People in the midst of the physical, emotional, and spiritual suffering of cancer often find themselves vacillating between despair and hope. Those closest to them are urging them to have hope and they desperately want to hope, but the existential reality of living with the losses and fears brought by cancer may leave them depleted of the energy necessary for the hoping process. A primary challenge for those in pastoral relationship with these people is to nurture hope.

As Andrew Lester points out, pastoral theology has for the most part neglected the future dimension of human time-consciousness and has therefore failed to provide "an adequate frame of reference for addressing the subject of hope."[5] Such a theological frame of reference is especially needed to undergird those in pastoral relationship with people experiencing cancer. These ministers, along with other oncology health care professionals, have often been so cautious of giving people "false hope" that they offer no hope at all. Instead of viewing hope as false or unrealistic, Jürgen Moltmann asserts that hope alone is realistic because it takes seriously all the possibilities of reality. Hope does not "strive after things that have 'no place,'" but after things that have 'no place as yet' but can acquire one."[6] The work of Lester, Moltmann, and Walter Capps provides a foundation for the theology of hope that informs the pastoral ministry presented in this book. Through expanding our theology of hope, ministers can develop creative ways of inviting people with cancer to experience hope in many forms.

This book will focus primarily on the use of sacred images and stories to overcome despair and encourage hope. I will explore ways in which a diagnosis of cancer challenges, and often changes, people's images and experiences of God. Spiritual responses to cancer, of course, vary according to each person's unique religious and cultural background and experiences. In an attempt to make sense of their experience some people may seek rationalistic or authoritarian religious systems. Others, wanting their religion to be a familiar and stable place within their otherwise chaotic experience, affirm more strongly the faith traditions in which they grew up. Fear and guilt may cause some to regress to more primitive, even superstitious beliefs. Others, finding their traditional belief systems inadequate to their cancer experience, begin a process of spiritual exploration and discovery. This book will illustrate ways in which ministers can serve as spiritual guides for people who are experiencing cancer, wherever they are in their spiritual journeys. By sharing in their existential search for meaning, we can help them revalue, reexamine, and transform their sacred images and stories in ways that bring healing.

Verbal and visual images of God form the foundation of spiritual experience. Sacred images reflect and shape people's deepest values. People who imagine God as uncaring and capricious will imitate these characteristics in their own behavior. Those whose image of divinity includes love and forgiveness will value these traits. The language and symbols people use in their attempt to express Ultimate Reality have a profound influence on their experience of themselves, others, and God. Elizabeth A. Johnson asserts that discourse about God is of "unsurpassed importance" because the symbol of God is the main symbol of a religious system, "the ultimate point of reference for understanding experience, life, and the world." Therefore, the way people speak about God represents what they believe "to be the highest good, the profoundest truth, the most appealing beauty."[7]

Sacred language and imagery may take on even greater significance in the experience of someone who is facing ultimate issues of life and death, as everyone does who is diagnosed with cancer. The names and symbols people use for God may increase the distress of the disease or may contribute to new discovery that leads to wholeness. Their God-images may increase their spiritual anguish to the point of despair or form the foundation for hope. If they imagine God as an Aloof Observer, indifferent to human suffering, or as a Random Destroyer, they may despair. On the other hand, images of God as Loving Presence, who suffers with them, contribute to hope. Many times people suffer unnecessarily because of limited images of God. For instance, in their illness they may focus mainly on the image of God as Great Physician, who heals those who follow orders. If they do not experience physical healing, they may then feel guilty that they did not do what was required. Images of God as a parent may also limit spiritual experience, according to the strengths and weaknesses of people's relationships with their own parents.

One of the creative, hope-enhancing contributions ministers can make to people with cancer is to guide them in exploring a variety of ways to express Ultimate Reality. As people struggle to make sense of their suffering, they need opportunities to imagine and name the sacred in new ways. Ministers can guide them to expand their imaginations and thus their experience of a Mystery far transcending their understanding, yet close and available to them. In the process, ministers can challenge people to let go of divine images that bring distress or that have lost their meaning, and suggest images that hold potential for hope and healing. One woman, struggling with leukemia, told me it was no longer helpful for her to think of God in human form, but she wanted some way to imagine God when she prayed. She said she felt God through music, that music made her feel "surrounded by a powerful force." Since her experience with cancer, she felt she was more sensitive to beauty than ever before. I suggested that she imagine divinity as Beauty, especially in the form of music. She responded, "I think you're expanding my horizons by saying it that way, giving me some extra sense or way of knowing."

One of my friends impressed upon me the importance of story to the hoping process. This friend and her husband had relatives who were victims of the Holocaust. She became a fervent advocate for Jewish people in our country and around the world who suffered any form of discrimination. Longing for me to understand her and her people, she would often talk to me for hours, telling me past and present stories of the Jewish community. It was clear to me that her passion for telling these stories came not from a desire to convert me but from a deep need for understanding. As a Jew in a predominantly Christian community, she did not always experience understanding and respect. Telling her story over and over to everyone who would listen gave her hope that she could contribute to justice for Jewish people in her community and all over the world. As a guest at her family's Passover celebration, I marveled at the power of the exodus story, told and retold and interpreted, to stir hope in the Jewish people, in spite of all the suffering they have endured.

In the same way that my friend longed for understanding of her experience, people with cancer often feel desperate for understanding. They welcome the opportunity to tell their stories to anyone who will listen. In the process of telling these stories comes relief from the isolation and alienation they feel. Whether or not they believe that the listener can change their cancer story in any way, they feel hope as they tell their stories to empathic listeners. In one study exploring hope in persons with cancer, a semistructured interview was used as a research instrument. One person affirmed that the interview itself not only helped him "review his beliefs" but also made him feel that he was "being treated in a caring, nonjudgmental way and that someone was truly listening to him."[8]

In my ministry, I find people not only eager to relate their stories to me but also enthusiastic about a wider audience for their stories. Everyone I asked for permission to use her or his experiences in this book expressed gratitude for the opportunity. When I told them that other ministers could learn from their stories, just as I was learning from them, they expressed feelings of satisfaction. Realizing that their stories had value, that they would make a difference to others, gave them hope that there was purpose in their struggle with cancer. With tears in her eyes, one woman said, "I feel like I'm helping ministers learn about my cancer experience. It's good to feel like I'm contributing." Seeing themselves as helpers and givers as well as receivers contributes to hope and healing in people with cancer. Talking about their experiences in an effort to help others contributes to relief of their own pain.[9]

In addition to giving sacred value to each person's stories, ministers contribute to the hoping process by assessing the future dimension of these stories. If someone's visions of the future do not give cause to hope, the minister can guide that person to revisualize the future in more hopeful scenarios.

The first chapter of this book provides its psychological framework by describing the emotional crisis that accompanies a diagnosis of cancer. In chapters 2 and 3 I establish a theology of hope as the foundation for the pastoral ministry illustrated in the book, and I make a case for using sacred images and stories to transform despair into hope. Then in chapters 4 through 9 the focus is on specific issues faced by people with cancer, illustrating the possibilities of the pastoral use of sacred images and stories to confront despair and nurture hope.

A diagnosis of cancer shatters a person's illusions of invulnerability and total control of life. In chapter 1, I draw both from narratives of people with cancer and from literature from the social and behavioral sciences to discuss the psychological crisis that accompanies a cancer diagnosis. The word "cancer" evokes fears of death, disfigurement, and physical dependence.[10] Psychological responses to this disease include depression, anxiety, anger, helplessness, and grief. Although the emotional reactions of people to cancer are unique to their own personalities and backgrounds, perhaps their most constant psychodynamic experience is grief over all the losses they sustain. People most often express the feeling of loss of control of their lives. Cancer may also bring loss of independence, job, physical endurance, friends, parts of the body, privacy, mobility, and even identity. Shame and low self-esteem often accompany all these losses. An existential crisis may come as questions of meaning, purpose, and value take on great urgency. This crisis may serve as the impetus for reexamination of religious beliefs and spiritual experience.

This reevaluation of belief systems and rituals often includes the exploration of familiar images that people learned from their religious traditions. Sacred images may help restore feelings of self-worth and meaning in people with cancer. Unfortunately, people's images of God often contribute more to distress and disease than to hope and wholeness. Many of those who experience cancer, and those in ministry with them, restrict spiritual experience by exploring no further than familiar, traditional images of God. In chapter 2 I illustrate ways in which ministers can guide people with cancer to face the positive and negative ramifications of their sacred images, affirming the life-giving images and letting go of others. Ministers may help people to expand their experience of Divine Presence by opening their imaginations to a variety of sacred images that contribute to healing and hope.

Narrative theology, along with a theology of hope, informs my exploration of the power of stories to enable persons to respond courageously to the psychological and spiritual dynamics of the cancer experience. In chapter 3 the narratives of people with cancer illustrate the challenge this disease poses to sacred stories and religious experience. Stories of religious experience in the past may lose meaning and power as people struggle with life-threatening disease. The cancer experience may keep them from extending their stories into the future. When I asked one woman to envision her future, she held up her hands directly in front of her face and replied, "All I can see is a blank wall." This chapter will demonstrate ways in which ministers can use the sacred power of stories to guide people with cancer to see a hopeful future or to rewrite distressing stories of the future. As they see the connections between their own stories and other sacred stories, including biblical stories, people can discover the value of their spiritual experience and its healing potential for the present and the future.

The examination of specific existential issues that challenge people with cancer begins in chapter 4. The uncertainty surrounding this disease is one of the most formidable challenges. Living with the unknown creates more anxiety for some people than any diagnosis or prognosis concerning their cancer. Since they are rarely pronounced "cured," most people with cancer live with the possibility of recurrence or spread of their disease. All the waiting involved with this disease creates stress and challenges hope. People with cancer seem to be constantly waiting—waiting for the next checkup, the next blood test, the next scan—waiting and hoping that the cancer has disappeared or at least has not spread. This chapter demonstrates ways in which pastoral interventions with sacred images and stories can help them refocus the future so that it is not dominated by the waiting.

In chapter 5 I explore how the hoping process can become dysfunctional in persons with cancer because of their feelings of responsibility and guilt. The increasing research on the connections among body, mind, and spirit has been a mixed blessing for people with cancer. On the one hand, this research may help them to feel that they can have some control over the course of their disease. But on the other hand, they may feel a burden of guilt from the inference that they caused their disease and bear a heavy responsibility for curing their disease. Other people feel guilty because of their belief that God has brought on the cancer to punish them for past sins, whether or not they can identify these sins. People may also feel guilty about the ways they are coping with the disease and about the burden their disease places on their loved ones. This chapter illustrates ways in which pastoral guides can challenge images of God that keep people with cancer bound in self-defeating guilt and can invite them to explore divine images that promote forgiveness and growth. Ministers can also help them understand their life stories from the perspective of their larger social context so that they can accept the limitations of their responsibility.

The social changes that accompany the cancer experience often leave people wondering where they belong. Roles and relationships with family and friends may change dramatically. If the cancer necessitates a loss or change of job, a sense of belonging in the vocational world may diminish. In chapter 6 I examine the social dynamics of living with cancer. Friends may withdraw because of fear, confusion about what to say, and anticipatory grief. Even family members, attempting to protect themselves emotionally, may distance themselves through denial. People with cancer may then feel rejection and shame. Through relationships that communicate acceptance, ministers can help people begin the journey from alienation to community. We can encourage them to accept limitations and to explore new possibilities in their closest relationships. One of the most effective pastoral interventions is to help them connect their stories with the stories of others going through the cancer experience, either through support groups or individual relationships. This chapter also demonstrates the pastoral use of divine images that empower people to develop mutual, empathic relationships. Hope for the future then quickens as they move from isolation to intimacy in relationship.

The physical changes that come with cancer also challenge the experiences of intimacy of people with cancer. In chapter 7 I discuss issues of embodiment and sexuality and their effect upon identity. Cancer and its treatment may significantly alter the bodies of people with the disease. Loss of hair through chemotherapy and loss of parts of the body through surgery are among the many physical changes. Loss of a breast, ovaries, or a testicle may affect sexual identity and functioning. Loss of fertility may also result from cancer treatment or cancer itself. Since body, mind, and spirit are intricately connected, physical changes and losses affect self-esteem and identity. The cancer experience may leave people unsure of who they are and unable to see any future for themselves. Pastoral guides can help restore hope by connecting these people's stories with other sacred stories of woundedness. In so doing, we may guide them to see themselves as more than their physical limitations. Another pastoral intervention is the use of images that bring Divine Presence close to people with cancer. One such image that offers possibilities of comfort and healing is that of Divine Lover, who suffers with them and thus understands their pain. The image of the Wounded Healer also inspires hope and power by inviting people to believe that, even in their imperfections, they reflect the divine image.

In chapter 8 I examine the ethical dilemma people with cancer face as they try to choose among treatment options. Realizing that the stakes are high in terms of survival and quality of life, they may agonize over their decisions concerning treatment. They often face these choices not only at the time of diagnosis, but repeatedly during the following months and years. They may feel overwhelmed as they try to understand the risks and benefits of many options for treatment. In addition to the conventional treatments of surgery, radiation, chemotherapy, and hormone therapy, there are experimental treatments and an increasing variety of alternative and complementary therapies. To complicate matters, their physicians may disagree as to the best treatment, and their managed care organizations may limit financial coverage for certain treatments. Amid all the confusion and conflict, pastoral guides can help people to identify their deepest values and to make their decisions based on these values. Inviting them to explore their sacred stories can facilitate this value-based decision-making process. Another pastoral intervention is the use of a variety of divine images to expand their thinking about the decisions they face. For example, the image of Divine Wisdom, serving as a partner in their decision making, may give them hope that their future is not determined by them alone. This chapter also explores ways in which theological ethics and medical ethics inform pastoral practice.

Perhaps the major challenge to hope for people with cancer is living with the reality that they have a life-threatening disease. From the time they are diagnosed with cancer, most people begin the existential struggle with their own mortality. The struggle intensifies if the cancer does not respond to treatment. If it does respond to treatment, they may still live with the anxiety of knowing their disease could recur at any time. Some people fluctuate between hope and despair as they move back and forth between remission and recurrence. Chapter 9 illustrates these spiritual dynamics, along with pastoral interventions that invite the reframing of hope and healing. The image of Divine Midwife may prove especially conducive to opening a person's imagination to see suffering as labor toward new life in the future. People may not experience this new life in the form of physical healing but in the form of healed relationships or recovery of lost parts of themselves. Pastoral guides can also invite people to draw hope from envisioning stories of a future that transforms death into life.

This book is designed for pastoral counselors and caregivers in medical settings, local congregations, and counseling centers. Although I have used the term "pastoral counselor" most often to designate the ministerial relationship, I hope that the theoretical and clinical material in this book will prove applicable to anyone in ministry with people experiencing cancer. In addition, the book is intended for the education of ministers in academic settings. The extensive use of case illustrations both develops my thesis concerning the importance of narrative theology in pastoral ministry and makes the book accessible to a wide variety of readers.

The clinical material for this study comes from my experiences of pastoral care and counseling with people who are struggling with cancer.

The setting for these experiences is a major medical center connected with the largest group of oncology physicians in the country. This book also draws from social science, behavioral science, and theological literature in describing and interpreting the particularities of this life-threatening disease.

The case material comes from my ministry with people in the hospital and out. I drew more extensively from my pastoral counseling with those out of the hospital. The people who came to me for counseling were those referred by health care professionals or friends, and those with whom I had established a pastoral relationship while they were in the hospital. These people enthusiastically gave permission for me to use our work together in this publication. Their names and some details have been altered to protect confidentiality.

In my counseling relationship with some of these people, I experimented with a structured guide to pastoral conversation (see Appendix B). In the initial counseling session, I found this guide to be useful as a spiritual assessment. Using this guide and taking notes on the responses also seemed to give people an added sense of the importance of the endeavor in which I had asked them to participate. They expressed satisfaction from contributing their experiences in this way. Through using this guide, I realized that a structured spiritual assessment may not only help pastoral caregivers and counselors focus our ministry but also contribute a sense of meaning and value to those with whom we minister.

This book comes with the invitation to others to explore the possibilities of sacred images and stories in pastoral ministry, using a variety of creative methods in a variety of settings. It is my hope that as we continue to expand our imaginations, we will increase our potential as ministers of healing and hope.

Chapter One

Cancer:
A Life-Shattering
Diagnosis

CANCER,
the word ricocheted around the room
and then lodged in my mind,
sending cold chills up my spine.
I flung it back out,
away from myself,
desperately stopping my ears
to its tormenting clang.
But the word reverberated
off the walls to the ceiling down to the floor,
moving up from my toes through the pit of my stomach and
bursting through my skull with its terrible truth.
Illusions of invulnerability shattered and lay in sharp, jagged pieces,
like broken ornaments under a brittle tree
the day after Christmas.

A diagnosis of cancer shakes a person's foundations. One person describes his feelings after diagnosis as "the blow in the stomach, the loss of breath, the struggle to think, the fumbling for words, the collapse of confidence, the pain erupting in the very bowels of one's body."[1] Despite advances in medical technology, the prolific development of alternative cancer treatments, and the steady increase in the number of cancer survivors, the word "cancer" still evokes images of suffering, dehumanization, and death. Cancer is the modern "archetypal symbol of misfortune and death."[2] When members of a cancer support group were invited to tell their initial feelings after hearing their diagnosis, a woman immediately responded, "I felt that I was going to die. The word 'cancer' meant death to me." A diagnosis of cancer quickly shatters a person's feelings of invulnerability and immortality. The physical crisis of cancer precipitates psychological and spiritual crises, often of the most profound dimensions.[3] A person diagnosed with cancer experiences an existential crisis as questions of meaning, purpose, and value surface with great urgency.

Perhaps the most constant psychodynamic experience of people diagnosed with cancer is grief and loss. The diagnosis of cancer constitutes the first loss. A healthy person suddenly learns that she or he is seriously ill. Almost all people diagnosed with cancer, regardless of age, react with disbelief. Hearing the diagnosis is shocking. Most people experience feelings of numbness, raw fear, and/or paralysis. These emotions may last for hours, days, weeks, or months.[4] In most cases, the emotional shock abates within a few weeks.[5] This common initial stage of grieving is especially pronounced in those people who had no prior warning of the disease.

In breast cancer support groups, women often tell of learning of the diagnosis and at first convincing themselves that there is some error in the tests. Since they have heard of other people who have been misdiagnosed, they appropriately seek a second and maybe a third medical opinion. If the diagnosis is confirmed, they may continue to feel that it applies to someone else even though they are rationally convinced of the truth of their diagnosis. At this stage they may describe a detached, out-of-body–like experience. They go through the motions of considering treatment options and perhaps beginning treatment, feeling that all of this is happening to someone else and that they are just observing.

Denial is a common initial coping strategy for dealing with a cancer diagnosis; it can be a healthy way of mobilizing hope and determination if used in a limited way for a short time.[6] Denial or minimization of the facts may be a protective mechanism against overwhelming anxiety, allowing people to gradually comprehend the painful news.[7] No matter how strong a person's denial, it is usually accompanied by feelings of panic. Some people vacillate between feelings of shock and terror or experience these and other feelings simultaneously at the time of diagnosis. The story of Rhonda, a woman in her thirties,[8] illustrates this wide swing of emotions.

The surgeon first drew a picture of a tumor in situ, contained in the ducts of my breast. Then as she started to draw the second picture, I cut her off because I didn't want to see the rest of it. I was terrified. She went on and told me the cancer was invasive and recommended mastectomy. I broke down, and my friends who had come with me tried to comfort me. I cried because I didn't know if I'd live or die and I was so worried about my family. I was scared I would slowly wither away, and they'd have to watch that process.

Then my friends and I walked out and just stood in the parking lot for a while. I was in total shock. My friends and I caravaned to the nearest bookstore to get the book the surgeon had recommended. Then I went home and called my mom. It was horrible knowing she was waiting to find out something. But I was still in shock.

After the mastectomy I went to see the surgeon to learn the results of the tests on the lymph nodes. She started talking about the reports showing malignancy and told me I would need chemotherapy. When she said the cancer might come back in the bone, brain, or liver, I felt myself leaving the room. At first I just felt dazed, like I was outside the window listening to the doctor give this news to someone else. Then it hit me and I started crying. I realized this was something I'd have to live with for the rest of my life. It was the end of the day, and the doctor and assistant left the office. My roommate and I were the only two people left in the office, and we just sat there for thirty minutes or more, just sat there dazed. Then we looked at each other and asked, "What are we doing here?"

Sometimes people's knowledge of cancer keeps them from the initial escape of denial. Wendy Harpham, a young physician, had treated too many people with cancer to be able to deny the stark reality of her own diagnosis. Although she felt the shock initially, she never experienced the cushion of denial.

The numbing shock, primal fear, and childlike helplessness and dependency stretched each of those first days into what seemed like a week. Facing my own mortality thrust me into a new dimension. Graphic memories of past patients deprived me of the strength and comfort that come from denial. I mentally telescoped my potential futures, focusing on the most frightening of what I had seen the past ten years. As my oncologist gently and dutifully outlined my treatment protocol, my mind reeled with the knowledge of the harm each drug could do, now or later.[9]

As the diagnosis of cancer becomes reality, grief over the loss of good health begins. Slowly or suddenly the realization comes that health, which had formerly been taken for granted, is vital to so many other things that have given life meaning. At this point people often move into another common phase of grief characterized by acute distress, turmoil, and depression. During this time they may experience preoccupation with disease and death, anxiety, loss of appetite, insomnia, poor concentration, and inability to carry out normal routines. A study of people with chronic illnesses, including cancer, found that those who were newly diagnosed had poorer mental health scores than those who had been living with their disease for longer periods.[10]

As people begin pursuing their treatment plan, the initial distress usually diminishes. Some, however, continue to suffer serious emotional problems. Jimmie C. Holland, a leader in the field of psychosocial oncology, cites a study revealing that 47 percent of persons with cancer had a level of distress equivalent to that seen in a psychiatric disorder. The troubling emotions may be triggered by medications used in the treatment of cancer or its side effects. If medications are not the cause of the psychological distress, Holland recommends some form of counseling.[11]

Cancer and its various treatments bring loss upon loss. Surgery may result in loss of body parts and perhaps sexual functioning. Prolonged chemotherapy and radiation treatments result in depletion of energy, making it impossible for some to continue functioning in their jobs. Even if the cancer is arrested, some people remain partially disabled and can never return to their former jobs. While some are able to take a leave of absence from their jobs, others suffer loss of their careers. Their roles within their families then shift as they can no longer provide financial support. Loss of the social network and status that accompany a vocation often follows. Feeling the loss of time is also common; people feel that they are losing time during all the treatments and that their lives may be shortened by the disease. They then feel the loss of expectations and plans for the future. One of the greatest impacts of the diagnosis of cancer is to throw into sudden question all the expectations and assumptions a person has had about what her or his life will be like.[12] Often accompanying all these losses are the deeper losses of a sense of purpose, security, self-worth, and even identity. After resigning from his job because of the debilitating effects of cancer, a middle-aged man commented, "I'm not sure who I am anymore. I guess I didn't realize how important my work was to my sense of worth."

As the person feels the full impact of all these losses, she or he usually moves through anger in the grieving process. People who grew up in families or churches that did not allow the healthy expression of anger often deny this feeling or give it a designation they feel is more acceptable. Instead of admitting anger toward God, people may say they feel confused that God let this happen or they feel life is unfair. People feel anger at their bodies for betraying them. Those people who have given their bodies the care recommended by experts especially feel this sense of betrayal. People with cancer also express anger at other people who are still healthy even though they have not taken care of their bodies, anger at physicians for not diagnosing them soon enough or for not guaranteeing a cure, anger at their families and friends for not understanding, anger toward the world for allowing this misfortune that is causing so much disruption in their lives, and anger toward God for causing or not preventing this disease. Rhonda says she gets angry "when there is mass confusion" in her life and when she can't "make sense of it all, when things are chaotic." She feels anger as she goes "through the utter hell of all the changes."A middle-aged woman diagnosed with lung cancer expresses her feelings of anger:

This just doesn't make sense. I never smoked and I always took good care of myself, and I'm the one who got lung cancer! What about all those people walking around out there healthy who smoke and drink and abuse their bodies? It's just not fair! I blame my doctors too. I kept having this nagging cough and went to my family doctor. He fooled around giving me antibiotics and decongestants. When I wasn't getting any better, I went to a specialist. It took him over three months to find the cancer! All that time the cancer was growing.

Sadness and depressive symptoms usually accompany or follow anger as people work through grief over all the losses they suffer with their cancer experience. Some people develop clinical depression with symptoms of insomnia, weight change, anemia, and decreased concentration. But most feel the sadness that is normal to grief. They may feel dramatic mood swings, buoyed by support of family and friends but then let down as the reality of their losses sets in. Charles, a man in his twenties, describes these highs and lows after his diagnosis of Hodgkin's disease:

A couple of weeks after I was diagnosed I had this spiritual high which I can't really explain. It felt like I had a conversion experience. I was so happy to have that gift, and I felt that the illness had brought so much peace and joy that I didn't really care that I had cancer. I always thought I would get over it though. Everybody said Hodgkin's was curable, so I never had a doubt that I would get over it. After a few months of this spiritual high, a depression started settling in. I wasn't working. Basically I was just having cancer and that was it. I was used to doing a lot of stuff, and I thought because of chemo I had to lie down all the time. I thought it was going to be much worse, so I didn't schedule anything. That inactivity led to the depression, I think. Also everyone else was moving on with their lives and I wasn't. I thought I wasn't as good as everyone else, going to prestigious law schools and working for accounting firms making a lot of money. I just really didn't like myself. I went through that for about six months and it was awful, the worst time in my life.

Then after I graduated, I got a job. Just getting back to work helped me. A combination of things helped me get out of the depression. I don't remember exactly when this happened, but Christianity really became part of me; I started assimilating the idea that Jesus loves me no matter what and I have to love myself. This absolute Love I was getting from various sources became part of me.

I do still have depression now and again, but who wouldn't from being sick. It's not because I hate myself. I still don't like it when I think I'm destined for a life that's not normal. I have to be with people my age; I hate being isolated more than anything. When I have to be in bed all day and sick, that's when I get depressed. I hate it. I keep beating myself up thinking I should be doing this or that. I still judge myself as worthless when I'm not doing something.

People going through cancer treatment often feel shame and low self-esteem as they experience physical changes. Cancer surgery may leave a person with physical disfigurement or bodily impairment. Chemotherapy may also adversely affect body image by causing loss of hair, loss of appetite, loss of weight, and loss of physical vitality.[13] Radiation may cause scarring of the skin, changes in appetite, and depletion of energy. These treatments, in addition to the cancer itself, may result in loss of independence, loss of privacy, and loss of mobility. One man diagnosed with colon cancer describes feeling the "loss of personal purity" and feeling that he is "perceived as contaminated." One young woman describes the humiliation and shame she felt from her lack of physical strength and from her loss of hair.

A cancer patient is humiliated by the lack of physical strength, especially in this day and time. Because the new rave is to be "disgustingly healthy" . . . one who is not in tip-top physical shape is made more aware of it than ever before. . . . I was so ashamed of my physical condition I overcompensated for it. . . . I was greatly disturbed by my hair loss. I sat on the back row of all my classes so that my fellow students would not have the chance to figure out that the reason my hair looked funny was really because it was a wig.[14]

One of the most common feelings that people with cancer express is grief over loss of control. A diagnosis of cancer strips away a sense of control and releases an assault of frightening possibilities, some of them known and some unknown. The unknowns about causes of cancer and the outcome of treatment magnify this loss of control. There is more loss of control when unexpected events happen in the course of treatment, such as more extensive surgery or chemotherapy than initially prescribed.[15] Recurrence of the disease after treatment and remission may heighten the feeling of loss of control. Especially if people feel that they have mobilized all their medical, emotional, and spiritual resources to fight the cancer, a recurrence often leaves them feeling helpless. A woman in her thirties who had been preparing for a marrow transplantation for several months learned the day before she was to begin the process that she was no longer a candidate because one of her scans showed metastasis to the liver. She lamented, "Now I don't know if there's anything I can do. I had put so much of my energy into the transplant, and now I find out that I can't have it. I think it would have been easier if I had never gotten my hopes up about this treatment." When determination and prayers and treatments do not bring the desired result, people may feel that there is nothing more they can do, that the disease is totally out of their control. Loss of the perception that life is just and controllable may cause great distress and even despair.

Debra, a woman in her fifties, described her feelings of complete loss of control when she learned she had breast cancer. She told of going to the oncologist for the first time: "He laid out the whole spectrum of treatment—from chemotherapy to surgery to marrow transplant to radiation. This just blew my socks off! I was scared to death about the future." An intelligent, logical woman, Debra tried to understand the cause of her illness. She thought that there must have been something she had done to cause the cancer. She seemed to believe that determining the cause of her cancer would help her feel more in control of it. What helped her most in dealing with her feelings of lost control was to become actively involved in helping herself through the illness:

As I started chemo, I got real busy trying to figure out what I could do to work with this problem. I started reading a lot of books to see what I could do on my part, as well as listening to what doctors told me. My antennae went up, and I tried to be alert to anything that would come my way. One of the first things that came my way was a support group; I'm sure that was an important part of my healing. I depended on that. Also when I was going through chemo, I listened to a guided imagery and affirmation tape every night when I went to bed. This tape also really helped me feel like I was doing something. I wanted to help myself through this.

Fear and anxiety are additional psychological dynamics of the cancer experience. Fear of the unknown is universal to human beings. People with cancer live with the unknown: the unknown origin of the disease and the uncertain prognosis. A cancer diagnosis begins a period of uncertainty concerning the future that may extend over many years. Cancer raises more questions than we currently have answers for. Often people feel frustrated and confused by the uncertainty of medical professionals. Doctors give them good news one day, confusing news the next day, no news for several days, and then bad news. This creates an emotional roller coaster that can be more stressful than simply getting bad news with absolute certainty. When cancer is first diagnosed, the fear caused by all the unknowns often produces more anxiety than fear of pain or even death. People commonly express relief after learning the results of a bone scan or some other test,

even if it shows cancer metastasis, saying that knowing what they face is easier than worrying about the unknown. As one person said, "At least I know
what the enemy is now."

In addition to fear of the unknown and fear of death, people with cancer often fear alienation, abandonment, mutilation, pain and suffering, and
dependence. Some have described themselves as the new lepers. One young
woman with Hodgkin's disease said she felt at times like a social pariah. Her
friends' fear of cancer often made them unable to interact with her, increasing her feelings of alienation.[16] People with cancer may fear that they
will no longer be loved and accepted by family and friends. In some people
the fear of abandonment is stronger than the fear of death. Some types of
cancer surgery, especially breast and prostate, elicit fears of mutilation.
Physical appearance and sexual functioning are threatened. Many people
with cancer express a stronger fear of pain and suffering than of death. One
woman said that when her oncologist started talking about all the treatments and their side effects "it was very, very scary." She wondered if she
were going to be strong enough physically to get through "all of that abuse"
to her body. For others, fear of dependency is most intense.[17] One high-
achieving young man said, "I don't think I want to live if I can't take care
of myself."

All these fears may leave people with lingering feelings of anxiety. Although anxiety may decrease after treatment, especially if remission is
achieved, some people with cancer become more anxious because they no
longer feel they are actively doing something to control the cancer. They
may worry that there are remaining cancer cells that they are not treating.
Even though they may feel relief over the completion of traumatic treatments, they miss the reassurance of the active involvement of health care
professionals. In a cancer support group one person said, "My friends think
I should be glad to be through with treatments. And I guess I am in a way.
But I have this nagging feeling that I should still be doing something about
my cancer, and I'm not sure what to do." With increasing media coverage
of research on the prevention of cancer, many people are anxious about
what they should eat, do, and think to keep the cancer from returning. After experiencing the trauma of a cancer diagnosis, many people live with a
free-floating anxiety that something else terrible may happen.[18] Those
whose treatment has not resulted in remission suffer from anxiety as images
of traumatic treatments, disability, and death remain in their minds.

The life-shattering experience of cancer reaches to a person's whole body,
mind, and spirit. The physical, emotional, and spiritual crises are inseparable. Kathy LaTour describes her experience with breast cancer as "ten years
of instant therapy sessions," taking her to the "very core" of her "existence."[19]
Michael Lerner, cofounder of Commonweal Cancer Help Program, refers
to life-threatening illness as "the Western form of meditation."[20] Western

culture puts greater emphasis on activity and achievement than on nurturing the spiritual life. Illness may provide the only opportunity for people to slow down, meditate upon their values, and review their lives.

The existential challenge for people with cancer is not just one of living or dying, but of evaluating what gives authenticity and meaning to life. The search for meaning can be the most difficult and rewarding experience of the cancer crisis. Meaning emerges through such things as pursuing a dream, experiences of Divine Presence, intense relationship experiences, and building faith in oneself. Hope will overcome despair if the suffering has meaning.[21] After completing her treatment, Rhonda said that her greatest fear is that she "may have gone through all this for nothing." She's hoping that an exciting new vocation will come out of her experience.

Many people describe the cancer experience as leading to a completely new life. Using language reminiscent of religious conversion, one man with stomach cancer says that his experience has been like a crucifixion, a death of an old way of life. He goes on to describe his rebirth to a new way of life—new zest for living, new attitudes, new interests, new desires, new loves, and a new sense of well-being.[22] People may describe experiences of rebirth on a physical, psychological, or symbolic level.[23] After a marrow transplant, some people describe feelings of death and resurrection. One person who received a transplant from an unrelated donor for the treatment of leukemia expressed these feelings.

I feel like I went to death's door and then returned. Maybe a little like Lazarus. There are many days I don't even remember because I was so out of it. Other days I wished I had never signed on for this. I thought death might be better. There were times when I really thought I was dying. I think I came close to what some people describe as an out-of-body experience. I felt myself floating on the ceiling, looking down at myself in the bed. Then I think I made a conscious decision to struggle to live. It would have been easier to quit breathing. But I remember making a conscious effort to keep on breathing. Now I feel that I've been resurrected, given another chance to live.

Many people who receive marrow transplants celebrate two birthdays: one on the day they were born and another on the day when they received their transplant, because to them that was another birth.

While few people feel grateful for a cancer diagnosis, many express satisfaction for the gains they have made through the experience. Cancer may become an opportunity for people to reevaluate their spiritual experience as they struggle with questions concerning disease and health, guilt and grace, despair and hope, death and life. One person remarked, "I would never have chosen cancer. And if I could go back now, I certainly wouldn't choose to have it. I wouldn't wish cancer on anyone, not even my worst enemy. But since I have it, I can see some changes for the better that probably wouldn't have come any other way." He went on to talk about reconciled relationships, deepening of friendships, changes in lifestyle, and renewed appreciation for the beauty of creation. Experience with cancer may provide the opportunity for healing that may include but goes beyond a physical cure. People with cancer may experience a profound change in their lives through an awakening to a deeper sense of their whole selves and of themselves in relation to others and to the world. This metamorphic process restores balance and a fuller experience of wholeness and integration.[24] One woman spoke of "recreating" herself after her cancer diagnosis and treatment.

One psychosocial study of people with cancer reveals that the ability to change goals and beliefs increases the possibility of successful coping with the disease. Changing from external goals, such as accumulating wealth and advancing one's career, to internal goals, such as appreciating friends and acquiring self-knowledge, may make it easier to sustain a sense of meaningfulness in the midst of the trauma of cancer. Internal goals can remain viable even when external goals are thwarted by the physical and financial constraints of cancer.[25] In the process of reevaluating goals, many people discover new gifts. After a diagnosis of cancer, Wendy Schlessel Harpham, a successful physician, discovered her talent for writing. She has published books that creatively combine her medical expertise with her personal experience of cancer.[26] Tina Fletcher, an occupational therapist, discovered new artistic gifts as she went through a marrow transplant. Now she is showing her paintings in galleries all over the country and finishing a master's degree in sculpture.[27] Kathy LaTour suggests that cancer may even help people find or engage their gifts.[28]

A life-threatening illness like cancer may arouse people's yearning to discover the truth of who they really are and what life is about. Cancer can be a catalyst for people to let go of comfortable illusions and become aware of their true values. People who experience cancer often discover that many things they once thought were important have no lasting value or meaning. In this process of discovery they come to know and follow their own inner wisdom and power.[29] Some people grow emotionally and spiritually through correcting long-standing problems and exploring areas of life that they had never had time for previously.[30] Charles said that his experience with Hodgkin's disease gave him a heightened awareness of spiritual reality. Before his diagnosis he had denied his emotional and spiritual life. The values that he had before his experience with cancer now seemed "ridiculous." He said, "I started assimilating the Christian value of absolute Love no matter what your material or worldly situation is."

Familiar religious systems and rituals may no longer make sense to people experiencing cancer and may cause more distress than comfort. People may examine for the first time the religious beliefs they had accepted without question. Internal spirituality may become more important than external religious forms. One woman in her fifties left the religious tradition she had practiced all her life because it felt discordant with her newfound inner wisdom. She commented, "I feel more deeply spiritual than ever before, but I can't go to that church anymore. The teachings just don't square with my experiences. Having cancer has made me feel that it's all right to take care of myself spiritually, so I choose not to go back. I feel most connected with God when I'm in my garden, taking part in creating beauty."

Many people going through an experience with cancer enjoy a heightened awareness of the beauty around them. Some talk about gazing with awe at a sunset or a flower in their backyard that they had never really noticed before. They savor these sights because they have suddenly realized that they might not be able to enjoy them forever. They feel more connected to all creation as they appreciate more fully the miracle and the fragility of life. They may experience a heightening of all their senses. One woman said that she had always loved classical music, especially that of Mozart and Verdi. Since her cancer experience, she said, this music sounds "a lot larger although not a single note is changed. It's bigger, fuller, more overwhelming than ever before. It makes me feel surrounded by a powerful force."

Often people do not pay attention to themselves and their own needs until confronted with cancer. Women especially may have built their lives on taking care of the needs of others and have never seen the virtue in taking care of themselves. Some have stifled their own needs to the point of total unawareness. Through the cancer experience many people realize that they have lived their lives according to the expectations and demands of others and that they have never really found their own voices. Not until she was diagnosed with multiple myeloma did Francesca Morosani Thompson, a forty-two-year-old orthopedic surgeon, discover that she had lived her whole life to fulfill the goals of others. She had become a successful surgeon, wife, and mother. She tried to live up to society's ideals for all these roles, and found herself exhausted and frustrated. When the workload was enormous and she was deprived of sleep, she shut herself off from her patients so that she could get her work done, but then she felt guilty for not living up to the ideal of a caring, compassionate doctor. She was also upset that she was not living up to her fantasy of being the great earth mother, always warm and giving. Through her experience with cancer she learned to feel at ease with herself and to take care of herself. Instead of trying to live up to everyone else's expectations, she now wants to satisfy herself. Her growth in self-acceptance and self-awareness has made her feel like a different person.[31]

The first challenge for anyone in a pastoral relationship with people experiencing cancer is to hear their stories of struggle and pain and hope in a way that validates and empowers them. As they feel our careful and compassionate attention to them, they will open their souls to us as they search for meaning. Each person's struggle and discovery of purpose will be unique. The discussion in this chapter of some of the psychological and spiritual dynamics that accompany a diagnosis of cancer is not an attempt to categorize people or to universalize the cancer experience. Just as the causes of cancer are complex, the emotional responses of people are complicated, individual, and unpredictable. There is no steady, orderly progression through these emotions nor a linear process to be worked through stage by stage. The emotions may come like a hurricane in tumultuous waves, like the steady beat of wind and rain, like raging and subsiding storms, and in countless other ways.

Pastoral relationships with people experiencing cancer present risks and opportunities. Because of the chronic nature of this disease, these relationships may last a long time. Pastoral counselors may find themselves struggling to balance being with and separating from the experience of these people. Some days I find myself achieving this balance, but at times I realize that I have internalized their experience too fully. Not only have I dreamed of the cancer experience of those I have pastored, but I have dreamed that I have cancer. This is a signal that I need to give myself time and space away from people with cancer in order to nurture my own spirit. I realize that I cannot be the best pastor to others if I cross the boundary between their stories and mine. I can be an empathetic listener and wise guide only as I live fully within my own story while giving caring attention to theirs.

The cancer experience opens rewarding opportunities as people meditate on life's deepest questions. It brings the people experiencing cancer and those in pastoral relationships with them in touch with mortality. Cancer has a way of shattering illusions that we will live forever. It brings us face to face with choices of how to spend our precious time. A reexamination of values follows. Those in pastoral relationship with someone experiencing cancer have the constant reminder of the importance of each moment and of living our moments and days to the fullest. When we hear people talk about their excitement when their sense of taste comes back after chemotherapy and about their joy in having the energy to take a walk with a friend, we learn a deeper appreciation of simple experiences we may have taken for granted. When we hear their stories of awakening to a deeper connection with creation, we feel more fully our interrelatedness to all life and our responsibility to nurture life.

Pastoral caregivers have the challenging opportunity to walk beside people with cancer not only as learners but also as guides as these people make new spiritual discoveries in the midst of life-threatening illness. This is a time when many people reevaluate religious beliefs and traditions that have been stifling instead of life giving. During this crisis people may be open to expanding their sacred images and spiritual experience. The extended time spent in pastoral relationship with people experiencing cancer offers possibilities for significant change. Pastoral guides may provide invaluable direction and support for people who are reexamining their beliefs and spiritual practice as they move toward wholeness.

Chapter Two

How Do I See God Now?
The Power
of Sacred Images

"Lord, Lord,
what have I done wrong?
I've tried to be strong
and keep your commandments.
Master, I know your demands are great,
and I hope it's not too late
for me to make amends.
Now I truly intend
to measure up."

Love draws me close,
calming my feverish soul,
tenderly speaking words of comfort,
    "You are my beloved in whom I take delight.
    Come, discover all I created you to be."
Now I feel my Everlasting Friend
    walking with me through pain and joy,
    leading me through meadows of green growth,
    filling my heart with songs of fresh hope.
Hand in hand we walk on
    into free-flowing streams of healing.

Sacred language and imagery are primary in shaping spirituality. Words and visual symbols both reflect and shape our experiences of Divine Presence. Biblical theology places importance on language, beginning with God's speaking the world into existence and moving to the image of Christ as the "Word." At the center of religious rituals are words and visual images. Words form the basis of pastoral ministry with people. In our counseling, prayer, and other rituals we name divinity. Our spirituality flows from the names and images we use to define Sacred Reality.

For people experiencing cancer, sacred imagery and symbols can make powerful contributions to the healing process. God-images affect what people believe about the nature of God and about God in relation to themselves. Images of God promote hope or despair, self-worth or self-abnegation. People who see God as a condemning Judge will feel less worthy and less hopeful than those who see God as a loving Friend.[1] Vital to healing is the belief that our lives have worth and that the One who created us loves us absolutely and unconditionally. Divine images that reflect unconditional, faithful love and care have profound healing value.

A vital part of pastoral assessment is the evaluation of each person's sacred images. We can make this assessment indirectly through careful attention to objects that have symbolic significance for persons. These symbolic objects may include religious pictures, icons, or statues that give comfort and meaning to people. Their religious language also reveals their concepts and images of God.[2] We can make the pastoral assessment of sacred images directly as well as indirectly. Through my experience I have discovered that people appreciate being invited to talk about their God-images. Many people going through cancer treatment welcome the opportunity to respond to questions about their concepts of God. Through questions about their images of deity, we convey respect and concern for them as whole persons.

Through our pastoral assessments, we will discover that many people have an ambivalent image of God as both loving and punishing. A diagnosis of cancer often brings the image of God as Punisher to the forefront, even though they are trying to believe God still loves them. The ambivalence in the biblical image of God may explain why many people in the Jewish and Christian traditions have difficulty imaging a God of unconditional love and grace. The biblical depiction of God as the source not only of blessings and joy but also of punishment and destruction instills the fear that the Source of our being is also in some way the Destroyer, that the One who nourishes us also seems bent on consuming us.[3]

Don, a young man diagnosed with leukemia, struggled with feelings that his cancer was God's punishment for not living up to the moral standards he had been taught in church.

DON: I just feel like God is punishing me. I've felt guilty about my lifestyle, but I guess not enough to change.

PASTORAL COUNSELOR: So you feel that's why you have cancer?

DON: Well, Chaplain, you know, I was pretty wild—drinking, sleeping around, doing drugs. I was never an addict or anything like that, but I experimented some. My doctor doesn't think this caused the cancer. He really doesn't know what caused it. But I can't help feeling that God's punishing me. I know I've also been taught that God forgives us, no matter what we do.

P.C.: But you're having trouble feeling this forgiveness?

DON (*sighing*): I want to believe God forgives me.

P.C.: Don, when you think about God, do you have any pictures in your mind?

DON: I'm not sure. Sometimes I think about some pictures I've seen at church. I haven't been to church in a while, and I feel bad about that too. But I remember a picture on the wall in one of my Sunday school classrooms. It's a picture of Jesus's face. He's not exactly smiling, but his eyes look so kind and loving. He looks very human in this picture. And one of the stained-glass windows at our church is the Good Shepherd. He's tenderly holding a sheep in his arms— I guess maybe it's the one that went wrong and got lost, and the Shepherd had to go out and bring it back. (*tears in his eyes*)

P.C.: Don't you think those pictures are there to show you something about God's love and forgiveness? How would you feel if you kept in your mind these pictures of God as the forgiving Good Shepherd and as the kind, loving face of Jesus?

DON (*crying*): I guess God doesn't do things to hurt us. Maybe God can forgive me.

People with cancer may for the first time examine their theological beliefs. They may have accepted the religious tradition of their parents without thought or question. They may never have explored the concepts of God and other doctrines taught by their religious traditions. The experience of cancer may raise questions about these doctrines or images, or, as in the case of Don, may lead people to see traditional images in a new and helpful way. Perhaps the way their family and community have taught them to see God no longer makes sense and may bring them more pain than comfort. They may begin to ask questions about who God is and where God is to be found in their experience. They may search for new sacred symbols more consonant with their cancer experience and more conducive to their healing.[4] For example, a person whose image of God is that of a Benevolent Ruler who controls everything and everybody may have difficulty reconciling this belief with the diagnosis of cancer. As people wrestle with issues of theodicy, they may even move away from traditional beliefs concerning the omniscience and omnipotence of God. People in traditions that teach God as the omnipotent Great Physician who heals those who have enough faith may shift to a view of God as Great Mystery when their faith does not bring the healing for which they have prayed.

People going through the experience of cancer may question the patriarchal images of divinity that their religious traditions have ingrained in them. They may begin to realize that their exclusively masculine images of God are not large enough and comforting enough to help them through this experience. Consequently, they become more open to feminine images of God. For example, a young man found the image of a strong and caring Grandmother God especially helpful as he was going through chemotherapy treatment. Although the predominant God-image in his religious tradition is Father, he has never felt the unconditional love of his father. As he was growing up, he experienced his father as demanding and stifling. His grandmother gave him total acceptance and encouraged him to explore his creativity. When he envisioned God as Grandmother, he found the confidence and love he needed to get through treatment.

After learning about the biblical personification of God as Lady Wisdom, a middle-aged woman felt empowered to decide among confusing treatment options her physician presented her. This sacred image led her to a new awareness of herself and her strengths. She exclaimed, "If Wisdom is a woman, then maybe I can be wise like her. Since she is a representation of God, I really can believe I'm created in God's image! Wow! That makes more sense now! Now I feel strong and wise enough to choose the best treatment for myself."

Our culture influences women to develop interpersonal connections, to be nurturing, and to be cooperative. It expects men to be independent and competitive. Although there is disagreement as to whether these traits are inherent or develop from socialization and there are signs that the socialization of girls and boys is slowly changing, these traditional associations with the feminine and the masculine continue. From her research, psychologist Lauren Ayers concluded that the internal forces our culture has traditionally associated with the feminine can be used to boost the impact of standard medical treatment for breast cancer. According to Ayers, skills that women in our culture develop, such as psychological insight and the ability to commit to relationships, can enhance the immune system and affect the course of breast cancer. Ayers comments on research that demonstrates the health benefits that both men and women realize from relationships with women. She concludes that a woman's typical behavior offers a means of emotional connection that lowers stress and enhances healing.[5] This research has profound implications for pastoral ministry, especially for our use of sacred names and imagery. Pastoral guides can encourage people to form supportive relationships not only with women but also with the Feminine Divine. Giving sacred value to relational skills traditionally associated with women may also support the fuller recognition and development of relationality in men and in our images of the Masculine Divine. As we eliminate stereotypes of the masculine and the feminine, we open new possibilities for nurturing, healing connections with human beings and with God.

Pastoral counselors have unique opportunities to guide people with cancer toward life-giving sacred images. Realizing that many people have ambivalent and even unhealthy images of God, we can gently lead them toward others. Through our naming of divinity in our pastoral conversations and in our prayers we can invite them to experience God in new, more health-enhancing ways. We can suggest scripture passages that picture God as loving and nurturing as a critique of passages that picture God as judgmental and threatening. Rosemary Radford Ruether's "prophetic-liberating principle of hermeneutics," using texts that reveal God's vindication of the oppressed to criticize texts that do not follow this liberating tradition, provides guidance in using liberating texts to criticize texts that oppress people suffering with cancer.[6] In addition, texts that reveal feminine metaphors of deity can balance those that present masculine metaphors. The common stereotypes of masculine and feminine traits along with the predominance of traditional masculine images of God reinforce many people's beliefs that God is more demanding than nurturing. We can offer healing from stifling stereotypes and traditions not only by balancing feminine and masculine divine images, but also by using tender masculine images, such as Good Shepherd (Psalm 23; Luke 15:4–6), and by using strong feminine images, such as Mother Eagle (Deut. 32:11–12).

The image of a divine Mother, like that of God as Father, has strengths and limitations for healing. This metaphor of a Mother giving birth to creation articulates the bonds of love and affection that bind us to God. Another strength of this imagery is that it expresses the kinship of all creation in the most intimate terms. It may help people experience the immanence of God more fully than other metaphors. Those suffering with cancer may find comfort in imagining themselves nestling into the sacred Mother's arms and drawing sustenance from her breast. Like the metaphor of God as Father, the metaphor of God as Mother carries limitations. For those people who have suffered abuse, neglect, enmeshment, or abandonment through relationship with their mothers, this metaphor will have little or no healing value. Even those who have not had such negative experiences may feel that the maternal image fosters infantile dependency. Pastoral counselors may help some people reshape this image into that of a divine Mother who desires her children to reach the fullness of their potential and who nourishes and guides them toward that goal.[7] The biblical picture of the divine Mother Eagle can serve as a model (Deut. 32:11–12). The mother eagle stirs up her nest to get the young eaglets out on their own. At first she takes them on her wings to teach them to fly and then swoops down to allow them to fly alone. She stays close enough to swoop back under them when they become too weary and weak to fly on their own. This metaphor shows God as encouraging people to grow and mature, yet as nurturing and supporting them when they are weak.[8]

Calvin, a middle-aged man diagnosed with lung cancer, had a strong determination to live. He used battle images when he talked about the cancer. From the beginning he was going to "fight this disease," "beat this thing," "win the war against this cancer." He wanted the most aggressive treatment available.

After surgery and a series of chemotherapy treatments, Calvin's cancer went into remission. About a year later Calvin began experiencing symptoms of shortness of breath and pain in his neck. Scans and X rays revealed recurrence of the lung cancer with metastasis to the bone. Calvin responded to this news with even greater determination to fight his cancer. He requested another series of chemotherapy treatments, although physicians gave him little hope of any benefit from these treatments. Calvin experimented with alternative therapies, including shark cartilage and various herbal teas. He explored the possibility of entering clinical trials.

Throughout this time, as he was in the hospital and receiving treatments in the out-patient cancer clinic, Calvin welcomed my pastoral care. Calvin had grown up in a conservative religious tradition and was currently active in a church as deacon, teacher, and chair of several committees. Every time the church doors were open, Calvin was there. He faithfully gave more than a tithe of his income to the church, believing this was what God required of him. The pastor, deacons, and other members of his church visited him frequently in the hospital. Although Calvin had no experience of women ministers and was not even sure he believed women should be ministers, he gradually moved from polite, superficial conversation with me to revelation of some deep hopes and fears. After a while, he began introducing me proudly to his doctors and friends, saying, "This is my chaplain."

Calvin felt that he was in the prime of life, enjoying his family and his career. After many years of working in a bank in a variety of positions, he had recently been named president. He was proud to have reached the pinnacle of his career and planned to stay there. As his cancer progressed, it became harder and harder for him to go to work. Because of increasing bone pain and respiratory distress, his movements were slow and laborious. No matter how bad he felt, he remained determined to go to his office every day. He told me that his vocational achievements and his ability to make a contribution to the world gave his life meaning. Calvin held the strong belief that God held him accountable for using his talents and successes for the glory of God.

When he developed an infection, Calvin at first resisted his physician's admitting him to the hospital. Calvin had to stay for several weeks in the hospital on intravenous antibiotics. His pain continued to increase until it was almost unbearable. He refused, however, to take the prescribed amount of morphine, because he wanted to stay as alert as possible. When I went to see him, he was extremely anxious and agitated. His wife was at his bedside trying to comfort and calm him. Calvin began by telling me that he was not going to give in to the cancer. This was only a temporary setback, and then he would return to work. He did not want to take too much morphine because he feared addiction and the slowing down of his respiratory system.

For the first time Calvin began to express fears of dying.

CALVIN: Chaplain, I'm in a terrible spiritual battle.

PASTORAL COUNSELOR: Can you tell me about how you experience this spiritual battle?

CALVIN: I know that Satan is trying to keep me from having enough faith.

P.C.: Enough faith for what?

CALVIN (*impatiently*):You know, enough faith to be healed.

P.C.: Oh, I see. You believe that your healing depends upon your faith.

CALVIN: Well, not entirely. I know there's God's will. But I believe it's God's will for me to be healed. I just have to have faith.

P.C.: Do you think perhaps there are different kinds of healing?

CALVIN: What do you mean?

P.C.: Healing may be more than physical cure. There may even be deeper kinds of healing.

CALVIN (*becoming more agitated*): I'm afraid I haven't lived up to my Lord's requirements. I just feel that I haven't measured up. I didn't smoke or drink or anything like that, so I guess I didn't cause my lung cancer. But I wonder if my life has measured up. You know the parable of the talents. I've been given so much, and I don't know if I've used it to the fullest. The Master demands a great deal from those whom he has given so much.

P.C.: So you see God as a hard, demanding taskmaster?

CALVIN (*talking faster but more softly as he labors to breathe*): You know the scripture, Chaplain. Jesus said that not everyone who says "Lord, Lord" will enter the kingdom. The Lord will only let those in who do his will. Many will try to get in, telling the Lord that they have done all these good deeds in his name, but the Lord will tell them to depart, that he never knew them. Only those who bear good fruit will get in. I don't know whether I've borne enough good fruit. You know that the Lord will divide the sheep from the goats, and I just don't know if my life has produced enough fruit.

P.C.: So you think it all depends on you and how much you've done.

CALVIN: Well, not exactly. Of course, I've also been taught about grace and I've taught others that salvation is by grace.

P.C.: Calvin, I'm sure you've taught the scripture, "For by grace are you saved, not of yourselves; it is the gift of God."

Calvin and I went back and forth for a few minutes quoting scripture. I tried to think of as many passages as possible on grace. With voice trembling and eyes filled with fear, he would counter with passages on what he interpreted as the "Lord's requirements." It seemed clear to me that Calvin's theology was bringing him more suffering than solace.[9] But I also realized that Calvin's spiritual needs would not be met by scripture quoting nor theological discussion. What he needed was the experience of grace on the deepest level to bring him ultimate hope.

I realized that Calvin's future story of judgment was based on his images of God as Master and Lord. These images suggest an all-powerful ruler holding people in subjugation and making demands that they have to meet or else suffer the consequences. No matter how far removed the images of Master and Lord are from their original contexts in feudal and slave-owning societies, they still carry strong connotations of demand and judgment. Calvin's divine images of Master and Lord were bringing him distress and despair, not healing and hope. Knowing that Calvin had had a close, healthy relationship with his mother, who was no longer living, I ventured the following pastoral intervention.

PASTORAL COUNSELOR (*moving closer and taking Calvin's hand*): Have you ever thought of God as a loving Mother who accepts and loves us no matter what?

CALVIN (*crying*): I remember how I could talk with my mother and she would always understand. I felt that she loved me even though I'm sure I disappointed her at times.

P.C.: She never would have told you to leave, that she never wanted to see you again.

CALVIN: Oh no, never. I know she loved me and accepted me completely.

P.C.: Surely if your human mother loved you so much, our Divine Mother loves you even more and would never leave you nor forsake you.

CALVIN (*sobbing*): I want to feel that love. Pray for me, Chaplain.

P.C. (*placing my other hand on Calvin's shoulder*): God, who loves and comforts us as a Mother comforts her children, may Calvin feel your comforting grace at the deepest level of his being. May he feel held in your arms of love, rocked in your peace, calmed by your soothing voice. Understanding Mother, as your complete love and acceptance flow like a refreshing river through Calvin, may he feel your healing of his deepest wounds of body, mind, and spirit. Wash away fears and restore within him the joy and hope of your presence, now and always. Amen.

After the prayer, I continued to hold Calvin's hand as his crying slowly subsided, his body became more relaxed, and he drifted to sleep. On subsequent visits, Calvin appeared more peaceful and expressed feelings of being loved and accepted, rather than judged, by God. He never experienced the physical healing he prayed for, but it was gratifying to take part in the transformation that took place within him as he experienced divine love.

The image of God as Friend holds important implications for healing. Sally McFague finds especially strong support for this metaphor within the Christian tradition. Jesus does not assume a master-servant relationship with followers, but a relationship of friendship (John 15:12–15). Of all human relationships, friendship carries the greatest possibilities of equality, freedom, mutuality, and companionship.[10] Regina A. Coll believes the metaphor of God as Friend is especially helpful because friends do not demand or command anything of one another, not even love. In relationship with God, our Friend, we can trust and expect the loving treatment one friend graciously shares with another.[11] The image of the Divine Friend may help people to let go of feelings that God is demanding something of them during their experience with cancer, something that they may not understand or may not be able to do. A relationship with the Divine Friend may bring them the companionship, mutual love, and healing power they need during the cancer experience.

In a cancer support group a young woman named Sarah sat quietly week after week, never speaking unless directly addressed. When other participants in the group asked her how she was doing, she would simply smile and say, "Oh, I'm fine." But it was obvious to the facilitators of the group, as well as the participants, that she was hurting.

The seventh session of this group focused on spiritual issues and cancer. At the beginning of the session, Sarah took her usual aloof stance as others talked of their spiritual experiences before and after being diagnosed with cancer. Some spoke of ways their cancer diagnosis had changed their images and ideas of God. Others expressed movement from belief in a God who is distant and judgmental to One who understands them and suffers with them. Several talked about feelings of anger toward God and then feelings of guilt because of their anger. In my role as facilitator and pastoral guide, I validated anger as a normal part of the grief process and affirmed anger at God as an important part of the experience of people of faith in the Bible. I referred specifically to the accusations against God recorded in the Psalms and to ways in which such anger led to a more authentic relationship with God.

At this point one of the other facilitators noticed that Sarah was weeping. As he reached out to her with comforting words, Sarah began to pour out her feelings of anger toward God. When Sarah was only ten years old, her mother had died of cancer. People in her family and at church had told her that her mother's death was God's will. Sarah thus developed an image of God as an uncaring Ruler in heaven who caused bad things to happen. Deep feelings of anger toward God grew within her, but she was not permitted to voice these feelings. Anytime she would ask why it was God's will for her mother to die of cancer, she got the response, "Don't ask why! God doesn't want us to ask why. It's wrong to question God." She came to see God as a Judge who would punish her if she did wrong. Along with this image came the haunting feeling that perhaps she had done something wrong that caused God to take her mother. For more than twenty years, Sarah had been stuck in these feelings of anger and guilt. As an adult, these strong feelings had kept her away from church. She had great difficulty praying and had almost given up belief in God.

With her diagnosis of breast cancer came a deep spiritual longing that she did not know how to fill. Now Sarah had a son who was eight years old, and she did not want him to have views of God like those with which she had struggled. She felt deeply confused about whether or not to take her son to church. She wanted him to receive support and comfort from a community, but she did not want him to suffer as she had with anger and guilt. Sarah especially feared that her son would learn the same ideas about God in church that she had learned, and would conclude that her cancer was God's will. Thus she agonized over what to tell her son about her illness, as her own spiritual struggle with her cancer diagnosis intensified.

Members of the group responded to Sarah with care and understanding, some revealing struggles they had experienced with their religious beliefs since their diagnosis of cancer. I suggested many ways they might see God, including God as caring Friend who understands all our feelings and even feels anger with us. I passed around cards with an artist's depiction of some of the biblical divine images, including the feminine images of God as comforting Mother and as Wisdom.[12] For most people in the group these were new ways of looking at God. Group participants talked about positive feelings stirred by these pictures.

After a guided meditation in which I asked participants to imagine God coming to them in any form that would feel comforting and healing, I asked them to share their sacred images if they so desired. Sarah was the first to speak. During the meditation, Sarah had pictured God in the physical form of a picture of Wisdom I had shown the group. Sarah imagined this figure as a Friend walking beside her, holding her hand, and saying to her, "I understand how you feel. I am here for you." Sarah expressed the relief and peace she felt through this image of God as comforting Friend, who understood her struggles. The feelings she had in the presence of this Friend were like those she was now experiencing with the caring people in her support group. She said that for the first time she saw God not as willing or controlling everything that happened, but as Someone who walked beside her as Friend and Companion. Although this image of God might leave her with questions about why things happen, she could more easily believe in this kind of God.

As she faced a marrow transplant for the treatment of her cancer, she felt empowered by her new image of God as Friend who would go with her. She also believed that she could help her son believe in this kind of God, even though this image might not provide all the answers to his questions about why she had cancer. To her, it felt more comforting to leave some questions unanswered than to live with an image of God as implacable Ruler and Judge. By experiencing the touch of her Divine Friend, Sarah felt confident that she and her son could make it through her cancer treatment.

Pastoral caregivers have opportunities to guide people with cancer toward healing experiences through our use of sacred names and images in support groups, pastoral conversations, prayers, and rituals. Many people see the historical role of pastor as including the power of naming the holy. When we are in ministry with people whose beliefs about God are bringing them distress rather than nurture, we can gently suggest other ways of knowing Sacred Presence.

Some people struggling with cancer may regress emotionally and spiritually, clinging to some image of God that feels familiar, however unhealthy it may be. A few years before she was diagnosed with breast cancer, Debra (see chapter 1) had begun a disciplined practice of meditation, drawing from several religious traditions. She described herself as "prayerfully going through a quest." After her diagnosis, she vacillated between this sophisticated belief system and her childish feelings of being punished by God. The following pastoral conversation reveals Debra's primitive feelings interspersed with her mature understanding.

DEBRA: When I was diagnosed, I was thinking of God as a punishing God. (*crying*) I think that you're given what you need to be given to grow, and unfortunately, some of us have to be hit so hard over the head to grow. I think our quest on earth is to become godlike.

PASTORAL COUNSELOR: You view God as hitting you over the head?

DEBRA: It's a wake-up call. (*crying*) Hard as it is to do, I think he gives you the tools to do it. I think God provides ways for all of us, and we zero in on what works for us. For me it's like a continually running program, and if I miss some information or something that's helpful at one spot because I wasn't focused, it will come up again. It's always there, everywhere. It may be in a conversation with a neighbor; it might be in a TV program or a song or something I'm reading.

P.C.: Debra, this sounds as though you feel that God is always there to help you on your quest. How would it feel for you to see God more as a Friend encouraging you to grow rather than a Punisher hitting you over the head?

DEBRA (*enthusiastically*): Yes, that feels better. I think that's right. Maybe like a spiritual guide I've had. He gently suggests things for me to read or new ways of seeing. And one of the ministers at my church has been this kind of friend to me. She listens and helps me to be more relaxed and also more open and awake to God's care. Maybe if I thought of God as like these friends, it would help me feel that God loves me. (*crying*) I do believe that God loves me.

P.C.: But you've had trouble feeling God's love?

DEBRA: Your suggestion of God as a nurturing Friend rings true. I have this recognition that I knew that, but I just didn't know how to say it. And I guess I didn't know how to feel it.

P.C.: Maybe naming God as Friend will help you experience the loving friendship of God.

A pastoral intervention that confronts a confused or diseased belief system may have powerful healing potential. Debra had been growing toward maturity in her spiritual quest. Her cancer diagnosis felt like a blow on the head; in her shock and fear she regressed to the primitive belief that God was hitting her over the head. But her mature theological concepts were still there so that she could readily respond to my renaming the Source of her growth through her cancer experience.

Many people experiencing cancer have difficulty feeling loved. Surgery, chemotherapy, and radiation may result in changes that make them dislike their bodies. Their self-worth may also be affected by changes or losses in vocational and family position. Because they have trouble loving themselves, they wonder if other people and even God can truly love them. Some people express the feeling of being betrayed by their bodies. Splitting their bodies and spirits, they may believe that God loves their spirits but does not care about their bodies. The sacred images of Healer and unconditional Love have important implications for healing. These images may serve to undercut the body/spirit split in some traditional religious views.

When extensive chemotherapy treatments for Hodgkin's disease along with prescribed steroids resulted in weight gain for Charles (see chapter 1), he struggled with his self-esteem. What helped him most was internalizing the absolute Love he was receiving from various sources. I invited him to elaborate on his experience of this Love and on ways he imagined this Love. He responded by talking about various sacred images:

Spirit is the overarching image for me, and then when I'm sick I image Healer. I think within that Spirit, God's a Healer. It is Love that is healing. Getting in touch with Love makes me feel whole; it sustains and heals me, gives me whatever I want from it. I also think of God as Mother; I think females are better at healing and more concerned about emotions. I also think of Jesus, because he was a person and he suffered like I do. Jesus understands me and loves me no matter what I do or look like, and I have to love myself.

The image of Jesus in his humanity, identifying with Charles in his suffering, helped him feel unconditional Love. Through this identification, Charles felt that Love became part of him.

Pastoral counselors have opportunities to help people with cancer discover that the locus of spiritual power is internal as well as external. When people are diagnosed with cancer, they often describe a feeling of being alienated from their bodies. This separation of mind and body is reinforced by the overlay of Greek dualism in Western religious traditions. Some traditional divine names and images may not aid people toward a healing reintegration of body and spirit. Nelson Thayer proposes the use of the symbol of Divine Presence in pastoral care to deepen openness and participation in the transforming process and to quicken the awareness of the sustaining, nurturing Spirit. Thayer believes that this symbol deepens our understanding of ourselves in relationship to God. We discover the depths of Being as we discover the truth about our own depths. In so doing we let go of images of God as ultimate Parent, Judge, and Ruler.[13]

The symbol of Divine Presence living within us affirms the sacredness of the integrated body, mind, and spirit. For people with cancer who may feel alienated from or ashamed of their diseased bodies, this affirmation may have great power. A middle-aged man commented, "I grew up in a church with a stained-glass window that had an image of God as an old man with white hair, a white beard, and a long white robe. Seeing that picture every Sunday, I visualized God as a man, as a father. Since my cancer diagnosis I visualize God as not having gender." He went on to say that the humanity of Jesus was now an important part of his picture, helping him to feel that Jesus understood his pain and cared for him. But he said he was not sure where the Holy Spirit fit into his picture. I raised this question: "Could it be the Holy Spirit within you giving you love and power to get through this experience?" He responded, "That just may be right. The other night I felt a Presence come into my room and then fill my whole body. A warm feeling went through me and then formed a protective shell around me." I asked him how this experience made him feel about himself. He replied, "Powerful, loved, protected, and accepted, deeply accepted."

Often in my pastoral prayers I use imagery to guide people with cancer to feel the Divine Presence within them. If they can discover that ultimate Being and Healing lives within them, then they can participate more fully in their own healing. In naming the sacred within people, I use phrases such as "Spirit of all peace and healing and power living within Carl," or "Source of abundant life and healing within Joan." In pastoral conversations I also encourage people to internalize efficacious images of deity. In the following dialogue my purpose was to affirm the healing power of abstract and concrete sacred images, supporting both external and internal sources of spirituality.

LOIS: I think that since I have had cancer my concept of God has grown; it's more encompassing than it was before. I rarely think of God in human form, even though I know Jesus was human. Jesus is no longer in human form although he works through human forms. Some of my favorite hymns that almost make me cry describe God as almighty and everlasting and encompassing and holy and immortal. My favorite psalm is "God is my refuge and strength."

PASTORAL COUNSELOR: It sounds as though it moves you to think of God as powerful and beyond our understanding.

LOIS: Oh yes! I always cry when we sing "Let All Mortal Flesh Keep Silent"; that's my favorite hymn. I picture this huge light and all these angels covering themselves with their wings because they're in the very presence of God and just can't look.

P.C.: You see God as Light, so bright that we cannot look.

LOIS: Brilliant Light, all-encompassing. We have to veil our eyes in this Presence.

P.C.: That's a powerful image. Are there other sacred images that help you during this time?

LOIS: I have an icon that I've hung beneath my cross where I do my meditations in my bedroom. It's the Virgin and Child; it's hand-painted with a silver overlay. I enjoy looking at it because it's so pretty. Another image that I carry with me is the Virgin of Guadalupe; flames surround her and yellow roses bloom at her feet. That has always been my favorite picture of the Virgin. There is no Child in this picture. And then not long ago I got to visit Fatima where the Virgin appears. I bought a rosary there that I use a lot.

P.C.: Those are important sacred images that you can see and touch.

LOIS: Yes, I'm a big holy site visitor, and I believe in rosaries and holy pictures.

P.C.: And it sounds as though you've included the feminine sacred in these pictures. The Virgin of Guadalupe surrounded by flames sounds like a very powerful feminine divine image.

LOIS (*enthusiastically*): Yes, you're right, you're right. I hadn't thought of it that way, but you're right. And I would turn to a woman as a comforting source. You're prompting me to see things in a new way.

For Lois it became increasingly important to bring the Divine Presence closer to herself through feminine sacred images. After going through high-dose chemotherapy treatments, she was left with many physical limitations. Among the side effects she suffered were decreased eyesight and energy level. An understanding employer made it possible for her to return to work in spite of her decreased capacities. But she found it impossible to continue her volunteer work. Her concept of herself as a good Christian woman included taking care of others. She commented, "It makes me feel bad that just because I'm not well I can't do anything. I feel bad not contributing something." Lois had earlier told me that her presence at work had helped other people who were going through cancer. People would come up to her desk and tell her about someone they knew who had been diagnosed with cancer. She would also receive phone calls asking for help. I suggested that by telling her story she was contributing just as much or more than she had previously contributed through her volunteer work. I also used the feminine divine image that was important to her to affirm the Presence ministering within and through her: "Lois, remember telling me about the Virgin of Guadalupe that you carry with you. She gives you so much power and comfort by her very presence. She is with you, and you are like her. Your very presence brings people hope and comfort." She responded, "I hadn't looked at it that way, but that feels true. Perhaps that's the reason I've been carrying her around with me."

Pastoral counselors have unique opportunities to guide people with cancer to face the positive and negative implications of their sacred images, affirming the life-giving images and challenging those which contribute to distress and disease. This is not always easy. Some people's images of God are so heavily ingrained that they cannot respond readily to pastoral suggestions of renaming the sacred. As Andrew Lester has put it, "deconstructing a narrative is more difficult to the degree that the narrative is embedded in the larger cultural worldview."[14] Likewise, challenging a sacred image embedded in the cultural worldview may be threatening and difficult. Masculine sacred images are deeply embedded in our patriarchal culture. The pastoral counselor who confronts these images, out of concern for justice and healing, may meet strong resistance. Even those people who are not involved in religious organizations have often imbibed from our culture the notion of God as "the man upstairs." Many people who have been active in their religious institutions all their lives, like Calvin, will find it difficult to reexamine traditional God-images like Master and Lord. The pastoral counselor's suggestions of additional images may not lead them to change the way they name God. But as with Calvin, a timely intervention may give them a different feeling about God in relationship to themselves.

The experience of cancer may bring with it a new openness to spiritual Reality. People may expand their thinking and naming of God to correspond to their new experiences. A pastoral guide's suggestions of new sacred images or names may open the door to healing and growth. With supportive guidance from pastoral counselors, people with cancer may let go of those sacred images that hinder their well-being, expand familiar images that have healing potential, and embrace new images that hold possibility for wholeness and health.

Chapter Three

Can I Still Hope?
Sacred Stories
That Bring Healing

We weave our lives with stories,
blending
> *wide and narrow,*
> *dull and bright;*
> *dark and light,*
joining
> *the pieces with*
> *unending threads.*
Our stories link creation.
Our stories bring revelation
> *of beauty unfolding on*
> *a holy tapestry.*

"Is there any hope?" The heart-rending question sounds through oncologists' offices, through chemotherapy and radiation treatment clinics, through hospital cancer units. After the diagnosis of cancer, one of the first feelings people express is fear about the future: "Do I have a future?" "How much time do I have left?" "What will my future look like now?" A cancer diagnosis has a major impact on a person's hoping process. Plans for the future may be deferred or aborted as the person's whole energy becomes focused on survival.

One of the most common feelings people with cancer express is that of loss of control. Among the important things they feel they can no longer control is their future. Whereas before they had felt they could set goals to accomplish in the next three or five years and make plans to accomplish those goals, they suddenly feel out of control of their future. Goals are the plot elements that help give structure to life stories. Often the cancer experience results in the loss of goals that had provided a sense of purpose. A psychosocial research study found that people can rediscover meaning through their cancer experience if they are willing to restructure their future to accommodate the cancer, changing their perception of the experience or changing their goals.[1]

Accompanying this loss of control is anxiety as those experiencing cancer live with uncertainty about the future. This is the reason some people insist that their physicians give them a prognosis of the time they have left, even though the physicians may be uncomfortable making pronouncements concerning what they cannot know for certain. Some people would rather know they have only six months to live than endure the anxiety of an unknown future. The inability to see the future or to see a better future leads some people with cancer to despair.

In recent years there has been an increase in research on the connection of body, mind, and spirit in healing. And there is growing interest in this study, as evidenced by the popularity of such books as Bill Moyers's *Healing and the Mind* and Larry Dossey's *Healing Words: The Power of Prayer and the Practice of Medicine*. Research in the field of psychoneuroimmunology (PNI) seeks to determine the relationship between the mind and emotions and the immune system. Although research studies to date have not proven a direct link between the hoping capacity and survival rate in people with cancer, belief in this link is common.[2] For this reason, people may ask their physicians not to tell them if their cancer recurs because they might "give up hope and die." Often family members who hear "bad news" while patients are in surgery try to keep this information from them because they believe they might "lose hope." Some people attribute their long survival with cancer to their hopeful attitude. In addition to the possible connection between hope and survival, hope has been associated with effective coping and quality of life.[3]

Hope in people with cancer takes many forms. While hope of survival is usually strong, people express many other hopes as they live with cancer: hope of change in relationships, hope of finding new purpose in life, hope of spiritual growth, hope of accomplishing goals, hope of quality of life with pain control, and hope of an ultimate spiritual life after earthly life. Some health care professionals who have a narrow view of hope focus more on helping people to face the facts of their cancer than on nurturing hope. As one woman recently diagnosed with lung cancer said to me, "My oncologist seems brutally honest. It's as though she feels she has an obligation to make sure I face reality. I do want to know my physical condition, but I don't need gloomy interpretations. Surely she can say something hopeful."

Helping people face their cancer realistically does not mean taking away hope.

Instead of considering hope unrealistic, Moltmann says that hope alone can be called "realistic, because it alone takes seriously the possibilities with which all reality is fraught." He goes on to explain his view of hope as not just taking things as they happen to stand, but as progressing and changing. Thus hopes are not "a transfiguring glow superimposed upon a darkened existence, but are realistic ways of perceiving the scope of our real possibilities, and as such they set everything in motion and keep it in a state of change."[4] Walter Capps comments on the movement in the past century from permanence to change as the context of theological affirmations. The focus then shifts from interpretation of what is to the question of which form change will take. The tense of theology is no longer restricted to past or to present, but includes the future. The question is no longer "Why?" but "which?"—which form will the future take?[5] People with cancer usually experience a similar progression. Although searching for answers to the question of why the cancer happened is important to the grieving process, moving to questions of what form the future will take is essential to hope. Emil Fackenheim comments that the only reason the Jews are still around after thousands of years of exile and persecution is their ability to hope for a better future. Their messianic hope has sustained Jews through unspeakable suffering.[6]

The hoping process in people with cancer is affected by the stories they tell and the stories they hear. A part of the existential search for meaning through the cancer experience is looking for patterns that give coherence to life. Through telling their stories, people with cancer seek to integrate their current experience into their life stories in an effort to discover hope for the future. People search their stories in an attempt to discover the reasons for their cancer, and they tell their stories to explore things they may do with their cancer experience. Woven into their life stories are religious and cultural stories that have shaped them. For many people, stories in the Hebrew and Christian scriptures provide either a conscious or unconscious background for their own stories. People may especially turn for hope to the biblical stories of healing. They also long to hear hopeful stories of other cancer survivors. Although statistics of the survival rate of people with their particular diagnosis may bring some hope, stories of individual survivors hold more power. For this reason many people choose alternative therapies that are supported more by testimonials than by scientific evidence. A story of one person who experienced healing through a particular type of therapy may contribute more to the hoping process than numerous statistical studies.

In *Hope in Pastoral Care and Counseling*, Andrew Lester thoroughly demonstrates the link between hope and what he creatively terms "future stories."

Lester defines future stories as the content we create to fill our future; these stories "make a significant contribution to the fabric of our core narratives, the tapestry from which our ultimate identity is woven."[7] Drawing upon narrative theory and the concept of temporality, Lester makes a convincing case for the importance of future stories to the hoping process. Narrative theorists have established that human beings discover meaning and form selfhood through structuring stories of the remembered past and the imagined future. Pastoral theology, basing its anthropology on that of behavioral and social sciences, has focused primarily on the past and present dimensions of human temporality. Neglecting the future aspects of time-consciousness, pastoral theology has failed to provide a framework for pastoral care and counseling to combat despair and nurture hope. Lester contributes a pastoral theology of hope based on the significance of the future dimension of human time-consciousness and then presents a model of pastoral care and counseling based on this theology. This model, especially the construct of future stories, contributes to my use of sacred stories in the pastoral care of people with cancer.

The narratives told by a person with cancer hold sacred value for that person's own spiritual development and for that of the listeners. Through an understanding of the revelatory power of stories, pastoral counselors can contribute to healing. Just as narrative is crucial to biblical revelation, stories told by people with cancer reveal possibilities for human life in relationship to Sacred Reality. Pastoral counselors can guide people to interpret their stories as sacred and to transform despair into hope.

People struggling with cancer may for the first time begin to reflect on their life experiences. Through telling their life stories, they may come to appreciate their holiness. James Conlon makes a strong case for the sacred value of stories:

> Story provides a pattern of meaning, coherence, and unity. The story is the primary vehicle for revealing who we are. Human experience is best portrayed as a narrative. A good story rings true, uniting us to what is sacred. It reminds us of our roots and challenges us to consider our destiny. It increases our capacity for reflection and empowers us to engage more fully in life. . . . Wherever liberating action is happening, stories are being told. . . . Our relationship to the divine is mediated through storytelling.[8]

Through telling their stories, people with cancer may be able to experience their spirituality better than in any other way. Spirituality is conveyed by stories because they speak the language of the heart. People tell stories especially in difficult times when the limits of human ability are reached. Storytelling provides a way of exploring the fundamental mysteries of life.[9]

In recent decades narrative theory has exerted a major influence on psychological, philosophical, and religious studies. Stanley Hauerwas and

L. Gregory Jones have collected essays on narrative theology that reveal the complexity and variety of applications of narrative, ranging from biblical hermeneutics to epistemology. They believe that narrative is central to theological and ethical reflection, even though some of its applications are conflicting and confusing.[10] Martha Nussbaum, in one of the essays in the Hauerwas and Jones collection, presents a fascinating case for the importance of narrative to a culture's emotional life. Narratives are essential to the process of practical reflection because they evoke emotional activity and because they are the sources of paradigms of emotion. The concrete judgments and responses embodied in stories more fully contain our deepest values and moral sense than the abstractness of theory; however, it would be foolish to rely uncritically on the data drawn from our experience of stories. Since stories contain and teach forms of emotion, emotions may be changed through rewriting or "unwriting" stories.[11] In an essay in this same collection, Johann Baptist Metz reminds us that not all stories carry equal value for pastoral care. While some stories reinforce unhealthy dependence and oppression, others aim at social criticism and liberation.[12] Pastoral counselors then have the responsibility of guiding people to evaluate their stories, to "unwrite" distressing or destructive stories, and to rewrite stories of hope and healing.

Taking a phenomenological approach, Stephen Crites claims that narrative is fundamental to human experience. He asserts that "the formal quality of experience through time is inherently narrative."[13] That is, human beings not only communicate past experience through stories, but also understand the present and future in the form of narrative. Crites sees two forms of human narrative experience: sacred stories and mundane stories. Sacred stories lie deep in the cultural consciousness of a people and provide the basis upon which people create a sense of self and the world. These stories, which are not directly told, connect people to the reality of their world. Mundane stories, which are directly told, form the means by which people articulate and clarify their sense of reality. Crites states that these distinctions are not meant to carry value judgments or religious connotations, but are simply a means to distinguish between the conscious world of the mundane story and the consciousness-forming world of the sacred story. Crites views sacred and mundane stories as inseparable, since mundane stories are implicit in sacred stories and draw meaning from sacred stories.[14] Because my emphasis is on this inseparability, I make no distinction between mundane and sacred stories, choosing to call all stories "sacred." Although people may give more authority to some stories than to others, my pastoral approach is to guide them to recognize the sacred value of the stories they tell about their lives.

Past and future stories often converge in the service of hope. Augustine, in his autobiographical *Confessions*, ponders the paradox of temporality. Although the present is all that exists, because the future does not yet exist and the past no longer exists, the past and future are existentially real. Augustine resolves this paradox by recognizing that the present includes our conscious awareness of past and future. Human consciousness links past, present, and future through memory, immediate awareness, and expectation.[15] A striking example of this time-consciousness is the experience of a woman after marrow transplant in treatment of leukemia. She had lost her sense of taste, a common side effect of high-dose chemotherapy preceding marrow transplantation. Three weeks after the transplant, her sense of taste had not come back. She told me, however, that she was eating her favorite foods because the memory of how they tasted and the anticipation of how they would soon taste made these foods enjoyable. Smiling, she said, "I'm having no trouble with eating, because I'm eating all my favorite foods. When I eat them, I can remember how they taste. And I think about how good they will taste again pretty soon. So it's almost like I can taste them now." Her memories and future expectations of the pleasing taste of these foods gave her hope that her taste would soon return, making even the eating of these foods in the tasteless present enjoyable.

Biblical stories often provide the vehicle for the convergence of past, present, and future. It is especially important to guide people who place authority in biblical stories to connect these stories to their own stories. Mark Jensen discusses similarities between the pastor's role as interpreter of scriptural texts and as interpreter of parishioners' life stories. Biblical texts and contemporary life stories share a narrative form. Both require the theological tasks of moving from the primary data to theoretical aids to interpretive suggestions. Both involve the shattering of inadequate, unhealthy interpretations. With pastoral support and guidance, people can let go of interpretations that no longer give coherence to their world or that do so only with the cost of self-destructive patterns, like addiction to work. Pastors can then become midwives as parishioners give birth to parables of liberation and growth.[16]

Telling their stories to pastoral counselors gives people with cancer the opportunity to integrate their current experience with past experiences and hopes for the future. Placing their life stories within a context of religious images and possibilities plays an important role as they cope with the uncertainties of cancer.[17] As they reflect on the meaning of their lives in the midst of a life-threatening illness, their own experiences with God may take on greater value than religious doctrines and institutions. For Donald Musser the Bible was "a book of answers and explanations " until his experience with cancer transformed it into "a storybook whose characters were trying to understand an ambiguous existence in the light of an Elusive Presence who had revealed to them some measure of truth and value." He began to find his story in the biblical tales as "grace shifted from an idea to be understood conceptually to an event to be experienced."[18]

By discovering the relationship between his story and biblical story, a thirty-three-year-old man named Bill was able to find meaning and hope through his struggle with lymphoma. He told me the story of his highly structured life before his diagnosis. He had been a man who was always in charge. A top executive for a computer company, he enjoyed prestige and financial security. He believed that his goal-oriented approach to work had led to his success in business. In his family life, Bill also liked to be in control. Although his wife earned an income as a professional educator, Bill's income was the primary support of the family. He kept the family books and handled all the financial affairs. Bill had also taken an active role in parenting their six-year-old son. Bill believed that his son's behavior problems had intensified during long periods of hospitalization that had kept Bill away from his family.

Bill had grown up in the Roman Catholic tradition; he appreciated the order of the rituals and doctrines of his faith. After his diagnosis of cancer, several friends began to talk to Bill about their beliefs concerning faith healing. These friends invited Bill to their charismatic church and brought him literature on healing. Because Bill so desperately wanted a cure for his cancer, he began to explore these beliefs. In addition, Bill received communion regularly from his priest and welcomed me as pastoral guide as he tried to integrate his religious background with these new beliefs concerning divine healing.

As his disease progressed, Bill lamented his loss of control of almost everything in his life. Not only had he lost his job and his physical strength, but he felt that he had lost his power of choice even in small things, such as his daily schedule in the hospital. He felt angry that he was "at the mercy of anyone who wanted to walk in the door." He expressed guilt that he was not reading his Bible and praying on a regular schedule in the hospital. He believed that he was "supposed to read the Bible every day to please God" and that he "must have faith if he were going to be healed." He wept as he told me that he could not always control his thoughts, that he often felt depressed and doubtful that he would get well.

His friends who had taught him about faith healing had told him that he needed to believe Jesus would heal him and that he should never allow doubts into his mind. Since he could control little else, this invitation to manage his thoughts had at first brought Bill some comfort. Just as he had worked hard at establishing structure in other areas of his life, Bill worked out an elaborate plan for controlling his thoughts. But this plan failed, and now he felt he had lost control of everything. He often thought of dying, and sometimes wished he could go on and die so that his suffering would end. His family was the main reason he wanted to stay alive. He told me that he could not let go of his wife and son and trust them to God.

Because Bill believed that his future story depended upon his ability to control his thoughts, he came close to despair. He could see only two scenarios for the future: he would be successful at controlling his thoughts and would be cured, or he would fail to control his thoughts and would die, leaving his wife and son in dire straits. My first pastoral intervention was to challenge his dysfunctional future stories with questions such as, "Do you think your future depends upon your controlling your thoughts? Where does God come into the picture?" When this intervention went nowhere, I tried the biblical story of the paralyzed man whom Jesus healed (Luke 5:18–25). Carrying the paralytic on a bed, some friends tried to bring him through the crowd to Jesus. Not able to get through the crowd, they went up on the roof and let the paralytic down through the tiles into the middle of the crowd in front of Jesus. Jesus' first response was spiritual healing. He forgave the paralyzed man's sins. Then Jesus healed the man physically. The paralytic did absolutely nothing for his healing; the story does not even indicate that he had faith that Jesus would heal him.

Together Bill and I interpreted this biblical story in connection with his own story. Bill felt almost completely paralyzed. He had lost control of many of his physical functions, of his finances, and of his family. At times he felt paralyzed mentally and spiritually; he could not concentrate or pray. Bill also identified with the paralyzed man's need for forgiveness. Bill felt he had hurt himself and others by having to be in charge of everything. He confessed that he had tried to play God and to control even God. He asked for forgiveness, honestly acknowledging that he might be using forgiveness as another way to control God so that his story would end in physical healing like that of the paralytic. We talked about different kinds of healing and about trusting God for whatever healing was needed for Bill and his family. I encouraged Bill to let me take him to Jesus as the paralyzed man had allowed others to take him. He had to do nothing but lie there.

After I prayed with Bill, he talked about feeling a deep peace as he rested in God's arms. He felt he was beginning to let go of his wife and son, trusting them to God's care. He would still pray for healing, but without feeling the need to prescribe the form that healing would take. Bill set more realistic goals, based on his limitations, but that gave him a sense of purpose. He modified his "either-or" thinking, his idea that because he could not control everything, he could not control anything. He discovered that he could still contribute to the management of the family's finances by using a laptop computer in the hospital. He also asked his wife to bring his guitar and music books to the hospital so that he could continue to develop his musical talent.

Stories help people with cancer by giving them back some sense of order and meaning. Feelings of regained control come as they structure and interpret traumatic events through the telling of their stories. When people can exert or believe they can exert control over their cancer, they adjust to it more successfully.[19] In a theory of cognitive adaptation to threatening events such as cancer, Shelley Taylor asserts that the adjustment process involves a search for meaning in the experience, an attempt to regain mastery over the event in particular and over life in general, and an effort to restore self-esteem through self-enhancing interpretations. Searching for meaning is an effort to understand not only what caused the cancer but also what implications it has. Regaining a sense of mastery after a cancer diagnosis often involves causal attributions that are perceived as no longer in effect. For example, if people believe that their cancer was caused by stress-producing conditions in their lives and they have now restructured their lives, they feel some sense of mastery over the cancer. People with cancer often restore their feelings of self-esteem by interpreting their experience in ways that give them positive feelings about themselves. These feelings may come through comparing themselves with others who are not coping as well with the disease or by finding benefits in the cancer experience.[20]

For people with cancer, stories facilitate all three of these adaptive processes. People attempt to discover meaning through telling stories of their precancer and postcancer lives, perhaps attributing a cause to the cancer and almost always exploring implications for their present and future lives. In telling stories of their lives before and after the cancer diagnosis, they often explore positive changes in lifestyle that are helping them master the cancer. Stories also help people regain their self-esteem after a cancer diagnosis. Because they have control of the characterization in their stories, they can depict themselves as adjusting well to the crisis and even making dramatic changes for the better.

As she told me her story, Rhonda (see chapter 1) struggled to find meaning through examining the spiritual implications of her cancer, to regain a sense of mastery through causal attributions, and to restore her self-esteem by interpreting her illness as bringing beneficial change to her life.

RHONDA: God got me out of a rut to lead me to a better life. I don't believe God is a punisher, but is Someone who gets your attention, a loving God who sees you to the other side. Everything works out for the best. I'm glad I got cancer.

PASTORAL COUNSELOR: You're glad you got cancer?

RHONDA: Well, not always. I get angry when things are topsy-turvy in my life, when there is mass confusion. But I'm not angry at God and not angry to be sick. I'm angry when I can't make sense of it, when things are chaotic. But I know why I got cancer.

P.C.: Why do you believe that is?

RHONDA: I got cancer because my walk with God wasn't right, and I wasn't in the right job. It was to bring a major change in my life. My job gave me too much stress and not much satisfaction. Maybe God is telling me to slow down and enjoy life. But I've been angry going through the utter hell of all the changes. I'm not good at handling the unknown. My guardian angel told me, "Don't interfere with the divine order. Just let it fall into place. It will all unfold. You'll see it unfold."

P.C.: I'd like to hear more about your guardian angel.

RHONDA: Before my surgery, I met this woman in my doctor's waiting room. She had white hair and was dressed in black. She looked so peaceful. She was the only person in the waiting room. The surgeon had asked her to talk with me because she had had breast surgery fifteen years ago. She just took my hand and said, "I know how you feel." She gave me assurance that she understood. During the next months when I faced scary things, like bone scans, she always called at just the right time. It was so weird. She visited me when I was in the hospital. She was always there for me. I'd never thought about guardian angels or whether they even existed. I'm absolutely convinced now that she's my guardian angel. There's a mystery about her, an aura that makes me know she's my guardian angel. The doctor can't believe she's still alive after fifteen years with the aggressive kind of cancer she had. It's like she's more than human. It gives me chills to tell you this story now.

P.C.: That is a powerful story. What do you make of it all?

RHONDA: She's helping me see that my life is going to be better now than even before I got cancer. I really needed to get out of that job and to change my workaholic lifestyle. I needed something to get me on track. I always felt there would be a calling for me. During the last few years I tried to discover what it was, but nothing had meaning. Now I'm finding more meaning. I love it when people ask me about my cancer experience. I look forward to using my experience to help more people—perhaps through public speaking and other ways. Living through cancer gives me great confidence. As my guardian angel says, something wonderful is going to unfold for me.

P.C.: How do you envision that future?

RHONDA: In five years I'll be dead or really successful. But I'm starting to believe exciting things are going to happen.

The main problem with such self-enhancing interpretations of the beneficial changes cancer had brought to her life was that they caused Rhonda to narrow her options to great success or to death. If she did not achieve the great benefits she anticipated from her cancer experience, she might feel she had no other choice than to die. The following intervention was intended to suggest that she might consider other possible future stories.

P.C.: You said that you see yourself in five years as either dead or really successful. It sounds as though you have to make changes that will lead to an exciting, successful life, or you will die. Are there no other options?

RHONDA: Maybe that is too extreme. But I know that I have to do something important with this experience. It just can't be all for nothing.

P.C.: You might begin exploring many possibilities for doing something fulfilling with your experience.

Rhonda agreed to dream about possibilities for her future and then to write them in her journal. When she came back for the next counseling session, she told me some of these future stories. She seemed much less frantic about finding that "something important" she was to do with her life. Having a variety of options seemed to give her the calmness and confidence to let her future "unfold," as her guardian angel had advised her to do. As was true for Bill, pastoral counseling guided Rhonda to transform her potentially destructive future story based on an oversimplified positive-negative dichotomy into expanded future stories filled with possibilities.

Narrative theology emphasizes the importance of stories in the reflection and the formation of a person's spirituality. Crites states that "the stories people hear and tell . . . shape in the most profound way the inner story of experience."[21] We "give shape to our religious experience through narrative structuring," Lester says, forming stories to make sense of our numinous experiences.[22] People with cancer often become more open to a variety of spiritual experiences that can be expressed only through narrative.

Before his cancer diagnosis, Charles (see chapters 1 and 2) had seen life through a rationalistic lens. He said that he "wasn't spiritual until cancer" and that he had "denied emotional life as well." When he was in the hospital shortly after his diagnosis, a chaplain came to see him. He tells of how impressed he was that this Catholic sister just came to be with him and did not try to convert him to any system of belief. The loving presence of this chaplain led him to begin to explore philosophy and religion on a cognitive level. He examined Plato's concept of absolute love and began talking with friends and ministers about religion. In the past he had felt alienated from Christianity because he had experienced judgmental attitudes from some evangelicals. One of his friends told him about Jesus' response to the judgmental attitudes of the Pharisees. Charles came to see Christianity in a different light. Attending a church where the minister had an "intellectual approach" also made Christianity more appealing to Charles.

During his cancer treatment Charles went beyond intellectual religious experience. He told a story of a numinous experience that brought profound change in the way he perceived the present and the future.

I was feeling very strange physically; all kinds of weird things were going on with my body. I was in bed, but I don't know if I was asleep or not. I started having the sensation of moving out of the bed and levitating over it. Then this something like a ghost, a scary white ghost with bony hands and a face that I don't remember grabbed me by the back of my collar and started flying. I was flying really fast with it, and I was really scared; I didn't know what was going on. The ghost looked at me and stopped midair. Everything stopped, and it just looked at me and said, "Don't worry," and something else like "because I'll be with you." But the main words I remember are "don't worry." That was all I remember. I was very touched by this experience, and I thought, "That was God!" This felt like my revelation from God: "Don't worry; I'm here." I really connected to that because I'd always worried about the future. It's always been a big issue for me. I just felt that God was saying to me, "If you just go from love, then you'll be fine; don't worry."

My pastoral role was to stand with Charles on holy ground, hearing his sacred story and validating it as revelation. His telling of this story and my hearing it connected us both with the mystery and miracle of his original experience.

About a year later Charles learned of the recurrence of his Hodgkin's disease. Again he went through feelings of anger, fear, grief, and depression. In fact, learning of the recurrence was more traumatic than the original diagnosis. He had felt that he was getting his life back to normal and was planning to get married in about six months. Now he had to face an uncertain future again. In pastoral conversation with Charles I explored with him the experiences that had given him hope in the past that he might draw upon to bring him grace for the present and hope for the future. I told him that I remembered the moving story he had told me a year before about his spiritual vision. Several weeks later Charles told me the story of an experience he had while doing meditation and visualization.

I was in a canoe. I had the same feelings as when I was suspended over the bed in my vision—really scared. I was going down a turbulent river in the canoe. I was going down the rapids, and it was scary. I had no

*guardian angel. The canoe took me to a field. A white figure approached
me. All of a sudden, I was reminded of that vision I had had during treatment, the one I told you about. I thought it was the same thing, the same
person coming to me. And God, or the Spirit Guide, or whatever, again
said to me, "Don't worry." Then I got back in the canoe and started going
down the river again. But this time I felt that God was in the river, and I
felt secure, even though I was lying in the canoe, going down the river
with no paddle, really in a very insecure and chaotic place. But because
I felt that God was with me and in the river, it was a secure trip, and I felt
safe. That was really powerful. God was in everything around me, even
though I was in the canoe in this chaotic, crazy, fast-paced world. I had
peace because I felt that God was with me. It was like the vision when I
was suspended and God said to me, "Don't worry; I'm with you." I had
felt secure after that experience. That vision has now become assimilated.
It's part of me. Now I can float down the river of my life with all the rapids.*

Entering into the narrative world of people with cancer, pastoral counselors have a rich repertoire from which to draw. In addition to challenging people to rewrite future stories, the pastoral task often includes
reminding them of their own sacred stories that have brought grace and
hope. Remembering the stories people tell us not only validates their worth
but also gives people the opportunity to reconnect with their past spiritual
experiences and to open themselves to new experiences.

Care in receiving and interpreting people's stories is another vital pastoral task. It is especially important to discern the elements in these stories
that give people distress and those that give them hope. People often feel
cautious about telling a "spiritual" experience that they fear will be misunderstood and that they may have difficulty even describing. It may take
time for them to trust pastors with these stories. Then they may begin with,
"I haven't told anyone this story, but since you're a minister, maybe you'll
understand."

Debra (see chapters 1 and 2) told me an experience that she had not told
anyone outside her immediate family. When she was going through
chemotherapy, she had what she called a "visitation." She saw a "dark face"
over her bed, and then she felt a sensation travel slowly down her neck and
shoulders, down through her arms and torso, and then down her legs all the
way to her toes. She said, "It's hard to describe the sensation, but it was beyond wonderful. It was flowing down my whole body. It was extraordinary;
it was a feeling that I had never had before. And I was just lying there, saying, 'Oh, thank you, thank you.' Then I asked, 'Who are you?'" The reply
that came to Debra was "Abba, Abba." She was puzzled because she had
never heard that name. A few days later when she was telling her experience to a family member who is a priest, he told her that Abba is another

name for God. Debra went on to tell me of the strong need she felt to tell this experience. And then with deep feeling in her voice, she gave me her interpretation of the experience: "I think that this visitation reprogrammed every cell in my body to think healthy. Instead of destroying itself, I think my body was being told—because I think every cell in the body is intelligent—to turn my cancer around. I think God was reprogramming my body for health." From that point on she felt that she would get well. She told her family not to worry anymore about her because she was going to be all right.

As Debra was telling me this story, it was obvious that she was reexperiencing some of the strong feelings she had had at the time of the "visitation." In fact, she said that as she told me the story of this experience, she felt renewed hope. My pastoral interpretation of her story was clear: her initial numinous experience and the telling of this experience were powerful contributors to her feelings of hope. When I expressed my appreciation and affirmation of her story, she felt an even stronger sense of validation. She told me she felt that we were together "doing something" for her healing. Whether this healing was taking place according to Debra's interpretation or in some other form was outside my ability to know or my need to interpret. My pastoral opportunity was to stand in awe with her in the presence of Divine Mystery.

Through the chaotic experience of cancer, when everything seems out of control, storytelling may help bring coherence and meaning. Through the structure of narrative, people discover order and purpose in their lives and in the world. Stories have power to restore hope because they put people in touch with Sacred Reality. The pastoral counselor has the opportunity to help people with cancer to discover the holiness of their own stories as well as to connect their stories with biblical stories and other stories to which they attribute divine authority.

Storytelling then becomes an important ritual available to the pastor. The ritual of telling and hearing stories requires sensitivity and skill. Often the pastoral counselor uses the skills of an interviewer, inviting people to tell the story not only of their present experience with cancer but also significant stories in their past and stories of the future they anticipate. Empathetic listening is vital to our attending compassionately and nonjudgmentally to these stories. Such listening is the key to helping people remember those times of grace in the past that can give them hope for the future. Exegetical skills then become central to our distinguishing the elements of people's stories that contribute to distress and disease and those that contribute to hope and wholeness. Pastoral guides can help people reframe past stories and rewrite future stories.[23] A pastor can make powerful contributions to the hoping process through the art of telling as well as hearing stories. Stories from scripture and from other sources help people see design at the foundation of life in general and of their lives in particular. Joining their stories with other sacred stories can reveal that there is purpose at the heart of the universe and that they are not alone.

Hope rekindles as people with cancer make new discoveries about themselves through these stories. Storytelling becomes a sacrament as Divine Presence is revealed in the midst of the struggles of cancer.[24] Like communion, stories connect people with a community of faith down through the centuries. Like the ark of the covenant, stories keep the Divine Presence alive through the wilderness of cancer. The holy privilege of the pastoral counselor is to participate in the sacrament of storytelling through giving and receiving.

In the chapters that follow, I will explore ways in which pastoral counselors can use sacred images and stories to challenge despair and nurture hope in people with cancer. I will identify how the hoping process can become dysfunctional because of specific psychological and existential issues that are part of the cancer experience. In these chapters I will also explore ways that pastoral counselors can help people transform despair into hope through reimaging the Divine, remembering hope-giving past stories, and rewriting future stories.

Chapter Four

What's Next?
The Waiting
Game

Sitting here alone,
   breath too clenched for sighs,
in a waiting room full
   of others waiting . . .
   aching to hear the word
   that will end the waiting.
Several years after the word
   that began the waiting,
I am still . . . waiting to live
   or living to wait?
I am still waiting and longing to know. . .
   Is there life beyond the waiting?
   Is there room in the waiting
      for life?

A diagnosis of cancer rarely involves a sudden, physiological crisis, such as often occurs with heart disease. In fact, people newly diagnosed with cancer frequently express consternation because they do not feel ill. It makes no sense to them that they have a life-threatening disease and still feel so well. They soon realize that they are dealing with a chronic disease that can hold them prisoner to fear and anxiety for years. They may find their lives consumed with waiting: waiting for pathology reports, waiting for the next treatment, waiting for the next bone scan, waiting for the six-month checkup, waiting to complete the first five years of survivorship and then learning that five is no longer a "magical" number. During all this waiting some people feel that it might even have been better to have had a heart attack that would have killed them quickly.

Health care professionals use the word "remission" more frequently than the word "cure." People with cancer are left feeling uncertain about the future, since no one can tell them how long they will be in "remission." They are left to deal with living under the stress of a potentially lethal physical condition. Donald Musser (see chapter 3) suffered a severe depression because his doctor did not pronounce him "cured" after five years of being free from the disease. He felt extremely disappointed that the doctor could not give him a guarantee against recurrence. He felt terrified when having a complete physical exam eight years after his diagnosis. After twenty years, he still saw his life through the window of his cancer experience.[1] After thirteen years of living with breast cancer, a woman expressed her fears of recurrence and her loneliness in living with these feelings: "It's difficult for my family and friends to understand my fear that the cancer might recur; they just can't understand my constant feelings of uncertainty. It's easier for them to put the cancer experience in the past than it is for me."

Richard, a three-year survivor of prostate cancer, tells of struggling not to dwell on his illness because he did not want to be like his mother who for the twenty years since her cancer diagnosis "has panicked with every little cough." But when Richard began to experience pains that he had not had before, his first thought was, "Oh my gosh, this is it. This is the end!" When he called and described his symptoms to the nurse, and she told him to come in right away, his anxiety increased. All he could think was "I'm going to die." Richard was, of course, greatly relieved when he learned that the pain was not due to a return of his cancer. After this scary experience, he understood his mother's fears of recurrence.

Learning to live with the unknown is one of the biggest challenges that cancer survivors face. In a book for cancer survivors, Glenna Halvorson-Boyd and Lisa K. Hunter use the term "limbo" to describe the state of uncertainty and insecurity that people with cancer enter with their diagnosis and remain in for the rest of their lives. The challenge, they say, is "to live fully and actively in the face of uncertainty and mortality."[2] People express the nagging anxiety of "limbo" through other images such as "living with a time bomb waiting to go off," "living on borrowed time," and "being on death row." Wendy Harpham uses the tale of the sword of Damocles to describe cancer survivors' experience of a looming threat that has the power to paralyze them. Damocles could not enjoy his lavish, luxurious surroundings because of a sword constantly suspended a few inches above his neck. In like manner, cancer survivors are perpetually menaced by the threat of death. The only way to escape is by confronting the realities of cancer and finding a way to deal with the fears.[3]

The "unendingness" of living with cancer and all its threats challenges the hoping process. Future stories may become dominated by the confusion of treatment options, the side effects of treatments, the possibility of recurrence, and fears of dying. Many people vacillate between hope and despair, feeling that they are on a roller coaster ride that they cannot control or escape. During all the waiting, their minds may jump ahead to scenarios that trigger fear and grief more than hope.

One of the challenges for pastoral counselors working with cancer survivors is to balance facilitation of grief work with guidance toward hope. Through all the times of waiting, people with cancer have much grieving to do. In addition to the physical losses, which can be traumatic, there are many intangible losses. Loss of security, loss of faith in the future, and loss of control are among the most profound. Underlying these losses is the loss of the illusion of immortality. Although we all know intellectually that we will die some day, emotionally we believe we will never die. People with cancer feel this illusion shatter, either suddenly or gradually. Anticipatory grief often arises as people for the first time see a future that includes their own death. Even though they may receive a good prognosis from physicians and even though they may be "cured" or in "remission" for twenty years or more, they never regain the feelings of invulnerability they had before the cancer diagnosis. These deeply spiritual struggles with issues of mortality challenge the hoping capacity. While walking with cancer survivors through the grieving process, pastoral counselors can guide them to develop hopeful future stories.

After more than a year with breast cancer in remission, Rhonda (see chapters 1 and 3) began feeling some pain in her back and in one leg. As is common for people in such situations, she immediately thought of a recurrence. But she was ambivalent about calling the doctor. She feared the bone scan as well as the return of her cancer. She desperately wanted to put the cancer experience behind her; she had tried so hard to move on to a life not dominated by cancer.

RHONDA: I'm afraid it's come back. But I keep putting off calling the doctor. I guess part of me just doesn't want to know. And I don't want to be running to the doctor every time I feel the least little thing. I just don't want cancer to run my life. And I'm scared to death of a bone scan. When I had one before, it was the most horrifying experience I've ever been through. The pictures took about six minutes each, and they took about five pictures on each side. I kept asking the technician to tell me what she saw after each picture. I knew she wasn't really qualified to read them. But she would say, "Oh, it looks good." When she got to my chest and didn't say anything and then went to the monitor and conferred with a person who looked like a doctor, I was terrified. I had had a pain in my chest, and now I thought they were seeing something bad. I had to wait several days to learn the results; this wait was awful. I was at my office when the doctor called and told me the tests were OK. Then I started crying and jumping up and down with joy and relief.

PASTORAL COUNSELOR: So it helped to find out that the pain in your chest wasn't cancer.

RHONDA (*laughing*): Yes, and I know you're going to say that I should go ahead and get a scan to relieve my mind about the pain in my back and leg. The other morning when I went to the bathroom, I passed a lot of blood. So I immediately began thinking, "Oh, my God, now it's spread to my colon!" After the panic, the main thing I felt was alone—so all alone. I have wonderful support from my friends, but they can't really understand how I feel. If I called them, they'd just tell me to get to a doctor, but they wouldn't understand the terror I feel. I didn't think I was afraid of dying, but all of a sudden it hit me how alone we are when we die. (*crying*) Then I felt waves of sorrow for all the women who have died of breast cancer and for everybody who dies—all alone.

P.C.: You're feeling painfully alone even though you feel support from friends. You feel that there's no way they can really understand your grief. They've not faced fears of dying, like you have. Is there any friend who can understand?

RHONDA: I don't know. I don't think so.

P.C.: Rhonda, do you remember telling me about your guardian angel?

RHONDA (*with tears*): How could I have forgotten about my guardian angel? Of course, she understands. She's been through this whole thing—the waiting, the terror that it's come back, the fears of death. And I've always loved that hymn, "What a Friend We Have in Jesus." I believe Jesus can be another friend who understands, don't you?

P.C.: That's one of the main themes of the Gospel story. The Divine Friend who understands and feels with you can come to you through your guardian angel and through Jesus. You are not alone now, and you will never be alone.

Through reminding Rhonda of a sacred image in a past story she had told me, I suggested a future story of hope-giving relationship to replace her feelings of despairing loneliness. I used the image of Divine Friend to help connect her experience of the understanding friendship of a woman who had been through breast cancer with her Christian faith tradition. This Divine Friend, in the flesh of her guardian angel and of Jesus, could understand her grief and fears of death because they had been through the same feelings.

Finding meaningful, hopeful life through all the waiting and uncertainty of the cancer experience presents a major spiritual challenge. While they are in treatment, it is often hard for people to see that life holds anything beyond the endless round of infusions and tests and trips to doctors and clinics. After they have completed treatment, their anxiety is often so high that they cannot imagine a future filled with anything but cancer. In the year after mastectomy, women may experience significant depression, anxiety, or sexual dysfunction that is related to fear of future recurrence of cancer more than to the operation.[4] Many people feel more emotional and spiritual distress after than during treatment. During treatment, surviving the physical side effects may take most of their energy. Also determination and a sense of purpose may keep them feeling hopeful. After treatment, they may experience confusion from their rapidly fluctuating emotions. Within minutes or hours, some people shift from feeling insecure to secure, listless to excited, hopeful to despairing, peaceful to anxious. Another source of confusion is the loss of the structure and focus that treatments provided.[5]

After the completion of treatment many people also feel confused by all the recommendations from friends, books, and the media. While they want to contribute to preventing a recurrence, people with cancer may feel overwhelmed by all the advice on diet, exercise, positive thinking, visualization, biofeedback, and other self-help techniques. They may become stressed trying to do all these things and then worry that this stress may cause a recurrence. The challenge is to find ways to integrate self-healing practices into their lives in ways that restore balance and purpose.

In a support group for breast cancer survivors, Joan expressed ambivalent feelings after finishing her treatment. Although she felt relief that she had survived her first year through surgery and chemotherapy, she felt a loss of the security that treatment had given her. Others in the group nodded their identification with her as she talked about her fears that she was no longer "doing something" to cure the cancer. Her life had radically changed with the cancer diagnosis. The year of treatment had given her some sense of structure and purpose, "something active to do." And now Joan felt that she was waiting, but she was not sure what she was waiting for. She was struggling to discover what to do next. She grieved for the time she felt she had already lost and did not want to lose any more time. With great intensity and anxiety in her voice she talked about trying to find ways to "put the pieces back together."

As other women in the circle told their stories, they reached out to Joan in her struggle. One woman told how shy she had been before her cancer diagnosis. She said that her experience with cancer had given her confidence. This confidence began to develop as she opened up to people in support groups and continued to grow as she volunteered at the hospital. She had gained new feelings of purpose and personal strength. Another woman likewise expressed the confidence she had gained through living with cancer; she felt that if she could live through cancer with all its uncertainties, she could live through anything. Another woman said that in her struggle to put her life back together after cancer, she had discovered the importance of her own desires and her own feelings. Before cancer, she had lived mainly to fulfill the needs of others. Now, for the first time in her life, she was taking care of herself and doing things for her own fulfillment. As the women talked, I could feel their concern for one another. With each word of hope, I could also see Joan's tension ease and her eyes fill with tears.

Sitting in that circle, I felt Divine Presence. At the end when it came time for me to interpret and summarize the group experience, a clear image came to my mind. I said to the group, "I feel awed and inspired as I sit in this circle, listening to your sacred stories and feeling the healing connections you are making with one another. As I feel the sisterly love and compassion flowing from each one of you, I feel that I'm in the presence of the Divine Sister." Joan replied, "Oh yes, I feel that too! I feel understood and completely accepted. You all have given me confidence and hope that I can put my life back together in new ways. This is a holy place."

Regaining a sense of confidence and control helps relieve the anxiety of living with cancer. Shelley E. Taylor's psychological study demonstrated that people's belief that they can control their own cancer and that physicians or treatments can control it are strongly associated with positive adjustment to the illness. People seem to be better off if they believe that they can do something to keep the cancer from coming back, even if this belief is disconfirmed. If they felt they could do something to control the cancer, and then had a recurrence, they would shift to something else they could control. Even illusions of control can be essential for coping.[6] Because hope operates in the realm of possibilities, it can remain in the midst of bleak present circumstances. Hope may be one of the few things some people with cancer can control. Controlling future stories can be a powerful aid to living with cancer. Hopeful future stories, even when they do not become reality, can be reframed and rewritten so that hope remains.

When Peggy was first diagnosed with breast cancer, she felt she had control over her disease. Even though her cancer had spread to her lymph nodes, she believed that through surgery, chemotherapy, and proper diet and exercise she could keep her cancer from returning. In her future story she was healthy and strong and vibrant. She expressed her belief that she "was not going to have cancer again." After a year in remission Peggy's cancer returned; it had metastasized in her bones and liver. After her initial feelings of shock and devastation, she sought the most aggressive treatment. At first her physician said that there was no treatment, not even a stem cell transplant, that would offer her much chance of another remission, so he did not recommend a transplant. But she persisted with him and with her insurance company until they approved the transplant, and she shifted all her hope for recovery to the transplant. During the months when she was waiting for a decision concerning the transplant, she expressed much anxiety to her doctor. He patiently and compassionately listened to her feelings, but one day he told her that even if she had the transplant, he could not give her any guarantee of remission. And if she did achieve remission, it would probably not be for long. He said to Peggy, "You're just going to have to find some way to live with this." She replied, "That's easy for you to say. How can I really live with the sword always over my head?"

In our pastoral counseling relationship before and after her transplant, Peggy struggled to discover a way to live with her uncertain condition. As she was approaching discharge from the hospital, she feared leaving the safety and security of the marrow transplant unit to go into an unknown future. She also expressed her anxiety that she had run out of options. If the transplant did not work, then what could she do? Her physician had offered no other treatment, except possibly experimental therapies.

Peggy's personality included a strong need for control. Even though her cancer had forced her to give up control in many areas of her life, she gained hope through feeling that she could do some things to control her cancer. Now that she had finished her last treatment, her hope began to wane with her feeling that there was nothing more she could do. I found her crying as she sat in her room waiting for her husband to come and take her home.

PEGGY: I guess I should be feeling happy that I'm going home. But I'm so scared. (*shaking and crying*)

PASTORAL COUNSELOR: It's scary to be leaving here.

PEGGY: What if this doesn't work? I try not to let my mind go in that direction, but I just can't help it.

P.C.: What do you see when you go in that direction?

PEGGY: Just more bad news. That's mostly what I've had from the beginning of this thing. (*choking*) I don't want to die yet. But I don't know what I can do now. I guess I've done everything, and now I just have to wait and see. I don't want to spend the time I have left like this—waiting and worrying.

P.C.: You want to do something else with your time.

PEGGY: Oh, yes. But I can't seem to get out of this, can't even control my thoughts. So I guess there's just nothing more I can do.

P.C.: Peggy, even though you may not be planning further treatment, there are many other things you are doing and can do. Every day since you've been here you've participated with me in prayer and meditation. And you've talked with me about finding new purpose in your work and your relationships. You also told me about your plans to gradually get back on your healthful diet and exercise program when you go home.

PEGGY (*laughing weakly*): Well, you know me. I have to try to do something. But I wonder if it makes any difference.

P.C.: What if I guide you through a meditation in which you imagine the difference you want it to make?

In the meditation I led Peggy to the sacred place she had previously described to me: a deck in her own backyard surrounded by trees and brightly colored flowers. I suggested that she visualize herself as she desired to be in the future. After the meditation Peggy told me about the future story she had been able to see. She saw herself focusing more on her internal than her external life. She envisioned herself working in a less stressful environment than the one she had previously worked in, and in a job where she was more creative. She also saw herself working "to better humanity in some small way: working for a cause, perhaps fund-raising for breast cancer research." Peggy found renewed hope as she changed her future story from "more bad news" and "waiting and worrying" to a story of spiritual and vocational fulfillment.

Sometimes the seemingly endless process of treatments and tests and checkups stunts the hoping capacity in people with cancer. They may lose their ability or desire to focus on a future story. Such was the case with Jack, a man in his fifties, whose colon cancer went into remission after surgery and chemotherapy, but then recurred after a few years. During the remission he continued to work, take vacations with his family, and make plans for his future. The news of the recurrence was quickly followed by more surgery and chemotherapy. After treatment the cancer went into remission again, but he had lost his confidence in the future. He had quit his job during his second round of treatment and had no will to return to work. Jack expressed no interest in making plans to travel with his family or pursuing his hobbies. Even though he had always enjoyed social activities, he withdrew into his home. Even after several years of remission, he rarely ventured out except for medical appointments. He seemed to be living from one checkup to another, afraid to plan anything until after the next test. The first year he had scans every three months; the second year, every six months. After three years, Jack was still saying that he could not begin to think about his future until after the next test.

In my pastoral relationship with Jack, I tried to help him regain hope. Whenever I would suggest the development of more hopeful future stories, he would respond that he could not make any plans until after his next scan. He saw no point in making plans because that test might show that the cancer was back. Finally I asked Jack to humor me by playing "what if," and he agreed.

PASTORAL COUNSELOR: Jack, what if your next test shows that you are cancer free just as your tests have for the last few years? What would you like to do?

JACK: If I could really believe I was cancer free, I'd like to travel. I've never been to France, and I've always wanted to go there. But I can't even think about that until I see what the test shows next month.

P.C.: Well, what if the test shows that the cancer is back?

JACK: That would mean I might not have long to live.

P.C.: How long?

JACK: Probably nobody could tell me that. But maybe just six months to a year.

P.C.: Is that enough time to go to France?

JACK (*laughing*): I see where you're going.

P.C.: If you do have just six months to a year, would you rather spend that time doing something you've always wanted to do or worrying about your next test?

Although Jack did not immediately plan a trip to France, he began to break his pattern of waiting, instead of living, from test to test. All human beings face the existential challenge of living fully in the midst of the unknown, but those with cancer constantly face it on a deeper emotional and spiritual level. The unpredictability of life moves from an intellectual truism to an experienced reality. The spiritual challenge is to manage fear and anxiety so as to move to new levels of wholeness and peace.

The first year after treatment for lung cancer, Rachel struggled with her constant fears of recurrence. Her anxiety sometimes reached the point of panic, keeping her from functioning on the job. She often had frightening dreams from which she would awaken in a cold sweat. She came for pastoral counseling to discover how she could use her spirituality to manage her fears. Rachel had previously been in a counseling relationship in which she had worked with imaging. Knowing that military images such as "bullets shooting cancer cells" did not resonate with her, she tried the image of sweeping the cancer cells out of her body. But this image left her worrying that she might miss a cancer cell as she might miss a crumb on a floor she was sweeping. So she had begun to explore the image of water washing away all the diseased cells. She felt reassured as she visualized water washing through her body, cleansing it of disease.

From me, Rachel sought spiritual direction concerning the integration of her Christian faith tradition with stress management techniques. Rachel told me about the evolution that she had experienced in her concepts of God. Anthropomorphic divine images no longer held meaning for her. She conceived God as disembodied Spirit, but she was seeking images that would bring God closer to her experience. I mentioned the biblical story of Jesus with the Samaritan woman, and she immediately recognized it. I reminded Rachel that Jesus used the metaphor of living water to describe the complete healing he was offering the woman.

RACHEL (*enthusiastically*): That's it! Living Water! The Water of Life! That's the symbol I've been looking for! Don't you see? That's the reason water came to me as a healing image. That's an image of holistic healing, and that's what I've been after.

PASTORAL COUNSELOR: Would you like me to guide you in a meditation using that image?

RACHEL: Oh yes! Please!

P.C.: Close your eyes, and begin taking deep breaths. Breathe deeply and slowly in and out. Breathe in . . . and breathe out . . . deeply and slowly. As you continue breathing in . . . and breathing out . . . slowly and deeply, let your imagination take you to a beautiful sacred place where you see in the distance a stream of water. Continue breathing in . . . and breathing out . . . slowly and deeply as you walk closer to the stream of water. Hear the soft, soothing gurgles of the stream as it flows gently down a hill. Walking along beside the stream, you feel a cool breeze blowing through your hair. You take a deep breath . . . breathing in the fresh, peaceful air . . . breathing out all fears. Thirsty, you reach down and scoop some water into your hand and take a drink. The water tastes clean and delicious, better than any other water you have ever tasted. You know that this is unlike any other water. It is Living Water . . . the Water of Life, and it is now flowing through your body-soul. Feel the Living Water . . . feel the

Water of Life . . . flowing through every cell . . . cleansing . . . restoring . . . healing. Living Water . . . gently flowing . . . gently healing . . . Living Water . . . Healing Water . . . Water of Life . . . flowing through your whole body-soul. As you continue walking along by the stream, you hear the sound of gushing water. Rounding a bend, you see a waterfall. You reach down and take another drink of the clear, pure water. Then you lie down on the grass beside the stream, feeling the Living Water course through your body, as the sounds and smells of gushing water surround you. Living Water gushing up to eternal life . . . Healing Water . . . Water of Eternal Life . . . within you . . . surrounding you . . . cleansing you. Feeling restored and cleansed, you stand up and take a deep breath . . . breathing in the peaceful Living Water . . . breathing out fear and distress. Slowly you begin to walk away from the stream of Living Water, knowing that the Living Water continues to flow through you, bringing healing and peace and eternal life. As you slowly come back to this room, know that you can return to the stream at any time to replenish your body-soul with Living Water.

The image of Living Water connotes the deepest kind of healing. Jesus told the Samaritan woman that it would become "a spring of water gushing up to eternal life" (John 4:14). This image suggested to Rachel a healing that could include but go deeper than a physical cure.

A growing body of psychosocial/spiritual research demonstrates a connection between prayer and meditation and healing of all kinds. Pastoral caregivers, according to a study of psychoneuroimmunology and its links to pastoral care, have "unparalleled opportunities to facilitate healing by combining the emerging science of PNI with the great spiritual traditions of prayer and meditation." The researchers believe that simple forms of prayer that quiet the "interior self by attentive breathing and relaxation" can take a person into a silence that has "healthy repercussions."[7] Deep connection with the Source of life and love holds immeasurable healing potential. At this level we experience release, forgiveness, grace, and gratitude that bring healing of spiritual and emotional wounds and oftentimes of physical illness as well. Centered in Divine Presence, we also transcend physical limitations and realize we are immortal. Larry Dossey claims that empirical studies on prayer's efficacy in physical healing carry profound implications for the nature of human life. The nonlocal nature of human consciousness, suggested in studies on prayer, indicates an aspect of human beings that is infinite in space and time and thus cannot die. Dossey states that "our intrinsic nonlocality constitutes an ever-present, Radical Cure—immortality—for the Big Disease, physical death."[8] Numinous experiences, along with scientific studies, make hopeful future stories possible for people with cancer, regardless of the course of the physical disease. A physical cure of the cancer, though still important, does not provide the only source of hope. Ultimate hope comes from the more certain "Radical Cure."

The chronic nature of cancer may simultaneously be one of its greatest curses and its greatest blessings. Few people living with cancer will deny the nagging fears, the devastating losses, and the existential struggle of this experience. At the same time many people feel a deepened sense of appreciation for each moment and a new spiritual openness through living with a potentially lethal physical condition. Waiting and living in the unknown territory of cancer carries great risks and possibilities. People may become overwhelmed with anxiety and grief and may even despair. Living with the uncertainty, insecurity, and unpredictability of cancer may, however, lead to profound experiences of gratitude and wholeness. These experiences may be brief and intermingled with grief, but they provide a refreshing oasis of hope. The waiting periods may provide the opportunity for heightened spiritual awareness and discovery.

Pastoral counselors can make a difference for people during the waiting game of cancer. First, through our centered presence in the midst of whatever uncertainties we are living with, we incarnate Healing Presence in our encounters with people. We contribute to holistic healing through "mirroring for another person a centered presence, a quieting of the mind and body, a trustful letting go in the presence of God."[9] Then through care-filled attention to the stories people tell of living with the unending unknown of cancer, we can help them to gain strength from the past and guide them to envision future stories filled with hope. In addition, we can lead people to experience Divine Presence through meditations focused on images that bring them healing, hope, and peace. In pastoral relationship, we have the sacred privilege of waiting with people as together we discover new life through intimate connection with the Spirit of all creation.

Chapter Five

What Did I Do?
Responsibility
and Guilt

What did I do wrong?
The question, like a stalker,
follows me relentlessly
nagging, demanding my undivided attention.

Running, hiding, taking another path,
thinking I have escaped,
I breathe a deep sigh.
But the stalker sneaks up from behind,
pulling at my sleeve, haunting my dreams,
poking me awake.
Finally I let out a loud yell,
"Forgive me, whatever I did."

Slowly a laugh begins to bubble up,
swelling irrepressibly,
shaking me from head to toe,
releasing tension and tears.
Through my laughter, I see
the stalker slink away.

People with cancer find many reasons to feel guilty. Religion, family, friends, the media, and society in general may contribute directly or indirectly to this guilt. Whether they believe they are being punished for past sins or suffering the consequences of stress and poor diet, many people feel responsible for their cancer. The more we learn about the causal relationships between lifestyle and cancer, the more reasons people find for feeling guilty when they are diagnosed. Whether or not their cancer has a direct connection with a specific behavior, such as smoking, they feel that they have contributed in some way to their disease. In addition, many people feel guilty for not being able to cure their cancer. Messages about all the things they can do to fight their cancer may only add to their guilt if they do not go into remission. People with cancer may also feel guilty that they are not coping with their cancer according to expectations, and that their cancer places a burden on those close to them. People may feel guilty not only for getting cancer, for not coping "appropriately," for the effects of their cancer on their loved ones, and for not being able to cure their cancer, but also for surviving it. They may suffer from survivor guilt when people they know die of cancer. All these guilt feelings may increase anxiety, or they may lead to health-enhancing change.

The increasing attention given to research on cancer prevention is a hopeful, much-needed balance to the emphasis on treatment. However, media coverage of this research often oversimplifies and may even distort the research so that we get the impression that prevention of cancer is entirely within our own control. If we just eat the right number and kinds of vegetables and fruits, get regular checkups, do the right kind of exercise, minimize stress, then we will protect ourselves against cancer. Our society holds us responsible for our health. Thus when diagnosed with cancer, people often feel a loss of self-esteem, guilt, failure, and shame.[1] In a breast cancer support group, one woman expressed these feelings: "I thought I had done everything I was supposed to do to prevent this. I eat a low-fat diet, and I exercise regularly. I get mammograms every year. I can't understand why I got this. No one in my family has had cancer. I don't know what's wrong with me that I had to get it. But I guess I did something wrong, or God's trying to tell me something."

Though they cannot directly attribute their cancer to any behavior, many people feel that God gave them cancer because something is wrong in their lives. They may feel that their cancer is the result of some terrible, possibly unforgivable, sin that they may not even be able to identify. Whether they have a concept of a harsh God giving them cancer as punishment for sin or a concept of a more benevolent God using cancer to get them to change some aspect of their lives, they feel a deep sense of guilt. William A. Fintel, an oncologist, and Gerald R. McDermott, a professor of religion who pastors people with cancer and their families, have found in their practice that a surprising number of people, either consciously or un- consciously, believe that cancer may be a punishment from God for past sins. Even though the biblical stories of Job and the man born blind (John 9:1–3) refute this explanation for cancer, people persist in this guilt-inducing belief.[2] Most people wonder why they have cancer, and punishment is an answer that comes quickly from primitive or infantile feelings.[3] In times of distress, many people fall back on the stern God of childhood encounters with religion.[4]

Often exacerbating this guilt is spoken or unspoken anger with God for causing their cancer, followed by the feeling that this anger is a terrible sin, perhaps blasphemy. After being diagnosed with bladder cancer, one man angrily said to me, "I didn't do anything to deserve this. I can't understand why I got cancer. But I guess it's wrong to question God, and I'll probably pay for this too."

While celebrating the continuing discoveries of the connection between mind and body and all the implications for healing that connection holds, we need to be aware of the potential for inducing guilt. There is another side of the coin of psychological or spiritual control over the development or spread of cancer. Sensational media reports and popular books often fail to locate the mind/body perspective within a context of comprehensive care, and as a result people may blame themselves for their cancer.[5] A burden of guilt may be added to the suffering of these people when they hear claims that the inability to love themselves or to experience love in their lives caused their cancer or that they caused the disease by not having managed their feelings and relationships better. The research on personality and cancer should be interpreted with caution because of the danger that people may feel guilty for bringing on their disease.[6]

When she was diagnosed with cancer, Debra at first felt guilty that she had caused the cancer by not expressing her feelings appropriately (see chapters 1, 2, and 3). In trying to understand the causes of her cancer, she studied the mind/body connection. She wondered if she had contributed to her cancer by stifling her feelings in order to accommodate others' feelings. Debra believed that her inability to express anger appropriately might have decreased the effectiveness of her immune system. Whether or not this interpretation was accurate, Debra was able to use it as an impetus for her emotional growth. Instead of staying stuck in guilt, she used what she had learned to take care of herself better and to express her feelings more fully.

Those who go to the extreme in espousing the mind's power to heal the body may, however, contribute more to distress than to healing. When mental and spiritual techniques are presented as concrete formulas for success, they may be more dangerous than helpful. The burden of success falls most heavily on people with cancer when they are least able to carry it because of the debilitating nature of the disease and its treatment.[7] For example, some people participate in programs that teach that by visualizing white cells ferociously attacking cancer cells, they can control the disease or eliminate it entirely. People who use such formulas and do not go into remission feel that they have failed. Thus these approaches carry with them the risk of imposing an excessive burden of guilt on people.[8] Likewise, people who rely on "faith healing" or "spiritual healing" may experience guilt if they do not achieve the healing for which they prayed. If they have heard claims that those who have enough faith or the right kind of faith will be healed, they will feel that it is their fault if they are not healed.

Cynthia, a young woman diagnosed with non-Hodgkin's lymphoma, received a marrow transplant from an unrelated donor. Recently divorced, Cynthia relied on her mother as her primary caregiver through the in-patient and out-patient phases of her treatment. Cynthia and her mother belonged to a faith community that emphasized charismatic healing. As Cynthia went through the grueling process of high-dose chemotherapy and the marrow transplant, they both prayed with great determination not only that Cynthia would be healed of the cancer but also that she would escape side effects.

A month after Cynthia left the hospital, one of the nurses in the out-patient clinic called me to see Cynthia and her mother because they were depressed. Cynthia was experiencing graft versus host disease, as do almost all patients who receive transplants from unrelated donors. But instead of understanding this as a normal part of the process of the donor's marrow grafting with her own, as physicians tried to explain, Cynthia interpreted this side effect as showing her lack of faith. Her mother also expressed feelings of guilt that her faith had not been strong enough and feelings of anger that God had not granted the miracle they had prayed for. Underlying these feelings was perhaps the fear that if their faith had not been strong enough to keep Cynthia from the bad side effects of treatment, it might not be strong enough to cure the cancer.

CYNTHIA (*voice quivering*): I guess I'm just disappointed and tired of all this. I don't understand. We've claimed all God's promises of healing and rebuked negative thoughts. But for over a month now I've had to come to the clinic every day and stay most of the day for transfusions, antibiotics, and who knows all the medications. I have zero energy, and now I have this terrible skin rash. (*showing me her arms*) They say I have graft versus host, and I'd prayed not to get it. I guess I just haven't had enough faith. I've let fears creep in.

PASTORAL COUNSELOR: From the stories I've heard from other people who've gone through transplant, your experience sounds like part of this long, difficult process.

MOTHER: But you know how hard we prayed that Cynthia's experience would be different. I'm disappointed and maybe a little angry that God hasn't answered our prayers, because we've done everything we know how to do. But I know I'm not supposed to question God because that shows lack of faith. It's not God's fault this is happening. It's ours, because we haven't had enough faith.

CYNTHIA: I wanted this miracle not just for myself but to show my father the power of God so he would believe. You know he's an atheist. I don't know why God hasn't granted the miracle we've prayed for. I guess it's just that our faith must not be strong enough.

P.C.: It sounds as though you believe your future depends on you and your faith.

MOTHER: The scripture tells us that if we have enough faith we can move mountains.

P.C.: Has this been your experience with God in the past? Has God always answered your prayers because your faith has been strong?

MOTHER: Well, not always. I remember a time when the bank was about to foreclose on a home my husband and I had been in for several years. We were having financial troubles. I was a believer then, but this was before I had much prayer life and before I knew much scripture. So I really wasn't praying about this crisis. I'm not sure I had any faith that things would work out. But I went to the bank officer and tried to refinance the house. The next day the loan officer called and said our application had been denied. I felt so frustrated and discouraged, and started to cry. Then I felt something or someone tell me, "Call back." So I called back, and the loan officer said she was sorry the application had been turned down and that rarely did the trustees reconsider, but she'd call the chair of the board. (*tears in her eyes*) Thirty minutes later she called back and said the bank would refinance our house. I just knew this was a miracle.

P.C.: That's a wonderful story! How does it speak to what you're going through now?

MOTHER (*crying*): I guess God has worked miracles even when I didn't have much faith.

P.C.: This miraculous experience you told me may relieve you of some of your feelings of responsibility. The refinancing of your house didn't happen because you had enough faith.

CYNTHIA: I've felt so guilty because I haven't had enough faith to get well.

P.C.: I hope your mother's story helps you to see that God's work doesn't depend on your faith.

CYNTHIA (*sighing*): That would be a great relief! I'll have to think more about that.

MOTHER: Thank you for reminding me of that experience. I know we still need to have faith but maybe we don't have to try so hard.

Through telling this sacred story in her past, Cynthia's mother began to reexamine a belief that was adding to the heaviness of the long, arduous process of caregiving. In hearing the story Cynthia found a seed of hope that might relieve her burden of guilt. If her physical condition depended upon God's work instead of her faith, then she would not have to feel guilty about all the side effects she was having from her treatment. Her future story could include her cure without all the effort she had put into working up "enough faith." And although I did not state the possibility of another outcome directly, I hope that my interpretation suggested that even if Cynthia did not receive the physical healing for which she and her mother so earnestly prayed, it would not be because of their lack of faith. In the hearing and interpreting of the story my goal was to validate its sacred and transforming value.

Pastoral intervention with people with cancer who feel guilty may involve challenging their sacred images. Robert, a young man diagnosed with leukemia, set high goals of spiritual discipline for the weeks he was to be in the hospital receiving high-dose chemotherapy. He planned a daily spiritual regimen of reading long portions of scripture, praying, and writing in his journal. In my visit with him at the end of his first week in the hospital, he expressed feelings of guilt because he had failed to read the Bible and meditate for the past few days. I suggested that the rigors of his treatment might have depleted his energy to the point that he could not continue this program. Robert countered that being sick did not excuse him from this responsibility, that God expected him to do this spiritual work no matter how he felt. I intervened by questioning his image of God.

PASTORAL COUNSELOR: Robert, how do you picture God?

ROBERT: I don't know if I've really thought about that, but I just know God expects us to at least read the Bible and pray every day, even if we can't do anything else. This is what I've been taught.

P.C.: It seems to be that you picture God as some kind of Teacher or Judge keeping score or grading you.

ROBERT: I guess so, in a way. Don't you think God expects us to at least pray every day? I feel so guilty, but some days I just don't feel like praying.

P.C.: Perhaps you might consider other ways of thinking about God and about prayer.

Several days later Robert told me that he had been thinking about my questions about how he pictured God.

ROBERT: After you left the other day, I kept thinking about what you asked me, about how I pictured God. All of a sudden a flame came to my mind—a large, glowing, warm flame. Then I realized that I did not light this flame, and I did not have to keep it going. It was just there inside of me, and nothing could put it out. I realized that all my plans of daily prayer and Bible reading had been not only to gain God's approval but also to keep God's mind on me so I would be healed. A great feeling of relief and peace came over me. Now I see God like this eternal flame inside of me. When I don't feel like praying because of the medication or pain, God will still be there and my faith will still be there, radiating without my having to tend it all the time. Even when I don't feel like praying, the flame of God or prayer or whatever is still in place in me and is working for me. Does this sound strange?

P.C.: It sounds like the picture of God in the story of the Israelites' journey to the Promised Land after escaping slavery in Egypt. You remember that the biblical story tells of God's taking the form of a pillar of cloud and a pillar of fire to lead the people through the wilderness. They didn't have to tend this fire or do anything to keep it going, but it was always there for them, just like the flame inside you.

ROBERT: Yes, I remember that story! I guess that's where my vision of God as a flame came from. Now I can just relax and let the flame lead me.

Robert had transformed his image of God from that of a Judge or Teacher whom he had to please to that of an Eternal Flame radiating within him. He did not have to keep lighting the Flame every day for it to continue working on his behalf. As Robert's image of God changed, the location of God also moved from external to internal. Now he could feel God "in place" inside of him, relieving him of the responsibility of "tending" his faith "all the time."

In addition to feeling guilty that they are not handling their spiritual or emotional lives according to expectations, many people with cancer feel guilty because of the effect their cancer has on their loved ones. They may feel that their cancer places excessive burdens on their family and friends. One woman said that she felt so guilty when she saw the pain her cancer caused her family that she "went around and apologized." Another expressed her guilt over the financial burden her cancer placed on her parents. In telling her cancer story she laments, "I feel extremely guilty because I am not always able to supplement their funds. I feel burdensome and costly."[9]

As strange as it may seem, people with cancer may also feel guilty for surviving. Like Vietnam veterans and others who survive life-threatening events, cancer survivors often struggle with survivor guilt, especially when people they know die of cancer. One man expressed these feelings: "I feel bad for doing well when my friend has died. Why am I living and my friend who is a much better person is dead? I just feel so awful for doing well. I know that may sound a little crazy." Although most cancer survivors know intellectually that their survival has nothing to do with the death of others with cancer, they may nevertheless experience feelings of responsibility. They may especially feel guilty if they have given encouragement to the person who died. One young man gave encouragement, reassurance, and advice to a friend's sister. When she died several months later, he struggled with his feelings of responsibility; perhaps he had given her the wrong advice. Family and friends may inadvertently exacerbate these feelings of responsibility. One young woman's parents discouraged her from seeing her aunt who was dying of lung cancer. They said to their daughter, "You can't go see Aunt Sarah. Are you trying to rub her nose in the fact that you survived and she won't?" Pastoral responses to survivor guilt include confronting the grandiosity of cancer survivors' feelings of responsibility for the death of others and helping them accept limitations. Survivor guilt may mask survivors' painful feelings of lack of control over their own or anyone else's mortality.[10]

Sometimes guilt in people with cancer may be a mask for difficulty in accepting the limitations of life. It may be easier for people with cancer to blame themselves for their own cancer or for the cancer deaths of others than to entertain the possibility that they have limited control over life. If they believe that they have caused their cancer, either by a major sin or even bad eating habits, they maintain a sense of personal control. If they can attribute a cause for their cancer, they can change the faulty behavior. Self-blame may also help people maintain their belief that there is justice in the world, that people get what they deserve in life.[11] Guilt may be a less painful emotion than the angst of living with unanswered questions concerning why some die and some live with cancer.

Even when guilt is misplaced or has no basis in reality, pastoral counselors need to respect and respond to people's expressions of guilt. These expressions tell us much about their relationships with God and with others. For example, if people believe their cancer is God's punishment for sin, we get a glimpse of their picture of God and of themselves. Bonnie Miller-McLemore reminds us to determine the appropriate and inappropriate character of guilt and to respond in accordance with this moral and spiritual assessment. It is important to assess individual responsibility in light of institutional sins, such as racism and sexism. Miller-McLemore follows feminist theology's analysis of women's sin in a patriarchal culture being more often self-denial than prideful self-assertion. Women who are ill may thus experience inappropriate guilt about personal responsibilities for loved ones. It is also important to distinguish between unhealthy, infantile, neurotic, self-defeating guilt and the "existential sense of human accountability for our lives in relationship to other lives and in relationship to that ultimate ground of being that all of us face when we consider our own deaths."[12] Guilt can become a catalyst for creative transformation.

Gloria sought pastoral counseling shortly after her diagnosis of uterine cancer. She told me her story of growing up with four older brothers, one younger sister, and one younger brother. Her father had left the family when Gloria was a baby, and her mother had been sick most of Gloria's childhood. Even though her brothers were older, her mother made Gloria responsible for the domestic chores. She also depended upon Gloria for help with the two younger children. Although Gloria liked school and felt she could excel, she did not always make good grades because she had so much work to do at home that she often did not have enough time for school assignments. As an African American in a predominantly white school, Gloria often felt the prejudice of classmates and sometimes of teachers. The pressures of home and school kept her from participating in social activities, so she felt lonely and isolated as she was growing up. She married the only boy she had ever dated right after she graduated from high school. After enduring five years of his abuse, she divorced her husband. For the next ten years she lived alone, choosing little contact with family or friends. The heavy demands her mother and siblings continued to make upon Gloria caused her to withdraw from them. She became so depressed that she did not reach out to make friends. Her doctor had given her medication for depression, but she quit taking the medication because of its side effects.

Gloria concluded her story by telling me that she believed her uterine cancer was God's answer to her prayer. When I questioned her about this, she replied, "I've been feeling so bad that I prayed for some way out. I think I would have killed myself if I had thought that God would forgive me. Now God has given me this way out." Gloria went on to tell me that she had chosen not to have surgery or any treatment that her physician had recommended, even though he had told her that she had an excellent prognosis with the treatment. Gloria expressed some uncertainty about her choice not to have treatment, and guilt that her death wish had caused her cancer. She asked me if I thought God would forgive her for causing her cancer and for refusing treatment. She wanted to know if what she was doing was the same thing as committing suicide.

There were no easy answers to Gloria's questions. The systemic sins of racism and sexism were intertwined with her individual responsibility for her life. The sins of her culture and family had stifled the development of her talents and her self-esteem. Long before she had consciously thought of killing herself, others had consciously or unconsciously killed parts of her essential self. When I asked Gloria how she saw her future, she replied, "I'll either die in a year or so from cancer, or I'll go on feeling terrible, wishing I would die." So in addition to addressing Gloria's immediate concerns about treatment of her cancer, I saw my pastoral challenge as helping Gloria revive parts of herself so that she could envision a more hopeful future story. I began by recommending that Gloria receive treatment not to satisfy the demands of a punitive God, but because her life was worth sustaining. I also encouraged her to attend an intensive weekly cancer support group as a way of making friends and discovering more about herself. At first Gloria seemed to comply with my recommendations more out of guilt than of hope.

After several weeks of sitting silently through the support group, she responded to the invitation of another group member to talk about her feelings. The understanding and warmth she received from the group seemed to give her new energy. In the next meeting she talked with greater animation, and after the meeting she exchanged hugs with group members. The next week she replaced her drab attire with a bright yellow pants suit and an attractive scarf to cover her hair, which was thinning from chemotherapy treatments. I heard her making plans with some of her new friends to meet for lunch and dinner. In the last meeting of the support group, she expressed her feelings of gratitude for the new life they had helped her discover: "When I got cancer, I thought my life was over, and frankly I was glad. I had been so depressed and lonely that I felt my life was not worth living. But you all have made me feel important and loved. I thought that cancer was my way out of life, but it's been my way into life." Gloria went on to say that for the first time in her life, she felt a sense of belonging and acceptance for who she was, not for what she could do for people. Through empathic connection with her new friends in the group Gloria began the process of redefining herself as a person of value. Now she would choose life not just out of guilt, but out of hope that her future held possibilities. The support group had become for Gloria a sacred community, empowering her to change her future story from one of despair to one filled with meaning and joy.

Although guilt may be less complicated when there is a direct link between a specific behavior and cancer, the feelings are no less painful. More than any other cancer, lung cancer tends to be related to certain habitual ways of life. Cigarette smoking is by far the most important risk factor in the development of lung cancer.[13] The increasing public education on the connection between lung cancer and smoking adds to the guilt of chronic smokers when they are diagnosed with cancer. Their loved ones may add to the guilt by reminding them that they have been warning them for years about the dangers of smoking.[14] Pastoral counselors need to be especially sensitive to the needs of these people who know that their guilt is justified. In a support group, one man with lung cancer expressed his feelings: "When people find out I have lung cancer, they give me this look like 'you got what you deserve.' Even nurses and technicians here at the hospital tend to dismiss me. Even if I caused my cancer, I'm still a human being. I still have feelings. I know I shouldn't have smoked. I'm sorry I've done this to my family and to myself."

Confession of sin begins the journey to forgiveness. The tendency of the members of the support group was to overidentify with the man's pain and to dismiss his confession with statements like, "None of us is perfect. You didn't mean to get cancer." My pastoral role in the group was to hear the man's confession and to take seriously his guilt over his self-destructive behavior. Implicit in his plea that he was "still a human being" was his need to have his feelings of guilt and responsibility taken seriously. I encouraged the group to acknowledge his guilt and to help him move toward forgiveness. I suggested that the experience of forgiveness could come not only from words of confession to those who had been hurt by his actions but also from changes in his actions. When he expressed gratitude to the group for their concern, I suggested that he picture God as this Caring Community who offered forgiveness and empowered him to make changes in his life.

Even though there are no definitive, direct connections between most cancers and behaviors, many people still feel guilty for getting cancer. It is important for pastors to hear people's confessions of guilt feelings before moving too quickly into introducing images of a God who does not punish through cancer.[15] As we have seen, people with cancer may also feel guilty for not being able to cure their cancer, for not coping with cancer according to expectations, for being a burden on their loved ones, and even for surviving cancer. Whether or not their guilt is justified, pastoral intervention needs to include attention to the dynamic of forgiveness. Since feelings of guilt and responsibility are varied and complicated, the experience of forgiveness takes a variety of forms.

When guilt belongs more to systems than to individuals, as in the case of Gloria, forgiveness may involve becoming aware of the role of institutional sin in the individual's life. In my pastoral counseling with Gloria I led her to see her life in its social context, so she could understand that she was more sinned against than sinning. Forgiveness for her would not focus on confession of her individual sins, but on acknowledging the sins of others against her. Forgiving them would involve letting go of their power over her. Thus forgiveness for Gloria would take a form similar to that which Marie Fortune recommends for victims of sexual violence. Forgiveness includes a letting go of victimization, such as through the following prayerful resolution:

> I will no longer allow this experience of violence to dominate my life. I will not let it continue to make me feel bad about myself. I will not let it limit my ability to love and trust others in my life. I will not let my memory of the experience continue to victimize and control me.[16]

A complex web of social sins, including the pollution of earth's environment, may have contributed to an individual's cancer. Though the individual may bear some responsibility for these systemic sins, they are larger than any individual. Forgiveness thus becomes a corporate as well as an individual experience. Pastoral interventions within support groups or other communities of persons with cancer may include not only discussions of systemic sins but also rituals for confession and claiming power for change. Effective pastoral interventions also focus on forgiveness as a reciprocal process involving both giving and receiving.

When Harold was diagnosed with prostate cancer, he determined to do everything in his power to fight the cancer. He chose the conventional treatments of surgery and radiation, as well as complementary nutritional and exercise therapies. In addition, he called "faith healers" around the country to pray for him, put his name on the prayer lists of as many churches as he could, and went to charismatic healing services. After initial treatments, Harold's disease went into remission. In less than a year, his cancer recurred in his liver. Though his physicians said there was not much more they could do for him, Harold was determined to move earth and heaven to be cured of cancer. He persuaded his oncologist to give him chemotherapy and sought out "faith healers" with greater fervor. The cancer continued to spread throughout his body. When I visited Harold in the hospital, he always asked me to pray with him for healing.

One day I walked in shortly after his oncologist told him that continuing chemotherapy treatment was futile. Harold greeted me with these words: "My doctor said he can't do anything else, but I'm depending on the Great Physician. You know how hard I've been praying for healing. It hasn't happened yet, but I'm going to keep praying. Pray with me." Harold literally meant for me to pray "with" him. Our prayers took an antiphonal form, marked by his refrain: "Thank you, Jesus. Heal me, Great Physician. Praise the Lord." That day in the middle of our prayer, I heard him blurt out, "I forgive you, God." There followed dead silence. Then Harold began to laugh. Beginning in soft giggles he tried to suppress, his laughter swelled to loud, uncontrollable guffaws. I joined in his contagious laughter. Finally his laughter subsided, and we had the following exchange:

HAROLD: That really takes the cake, doesn't it? That I would be offering God forgiveness. I know God was glad to hear that! (*laughing*) I don't know where that came from.

PASTORAL COUNSELOR: I imagine that God was glad and that God joined our laughter. Maybe you need to forgive God for not being your Great Physician.

HAROLD: I guess I can't make God be that. But I guess I am disappointed because I've prayed so long and hard and done everything I know to do to get well.

P.C.: You have, Harold. Maybe you didn't experience God as Great Physician today, but perhaps as something or someone else.

HAROLD (*laughing*): Maybe as a Laughing Companion. I didn't feel God got mad when I said "I forgive you" and laughed right in the middle of our prayer. I felt God laughing with us.

For people with cancer, forgiveness may involve accepting the limitations of human life. In this process they may need to forgive God, life, and their own bodies for letting them down. It may be easier to feel guilty for causing their cancer through some behavior that can be changed, even if the guilt is unjustified, than to feel anxiety over their limited control of cancer. Confessing some specific sin may be less painful than acknowledging limitations and vulnerability and mortality. It may be simpler for persons with cancer to try to program God to be their Great Physician than to trust themselves to the Great Mystery.

Experiencing forgiveness is among the profound spiritual challenges persons with cancer face. Feelings of guilt and responsibility bombard them from many directions and in a variety of forms. Pastoral interventions need to be informed by both the primitive and the complex nature of this guilt. Hearing confessions and offering forgiveness may provide comfort when people express the feeling that cancer is God's punishment for their sins. But when guilt masks feelings of angst over life's ambiguities and limitations, the process of forgiveness becomes more complex. As pastoral guides we can challenge images of God that keep people mired in unhealthy, self-defeating guilt and invite them to move toward divine images that promote growth and discovery. We can help people understand their life stories not only from the perspective of their individual responsibility but also in the context of social evil. Entering into their stories, we can feel with them the anxiety of human limitations and the relief that comes from forgiving whoever or whatever is responsible for these limitations. It is also our holy privilege to stimulate the imagination to create future stories filled with joy and hope and grace.

Chapter Six

Where Do I Belong? The Social Consequences

Dancing in the circle,
spinning with delight,
I moved in sync with all the others
in the magic ring
of love and life.

Suddenly the dancing stopped.
The circle broke
as I fell back alone, outside,
the ancient chant "unclean, unclean"
drumming in my head.

Staggering up, I heard
another sound and opened my eyes
to see another circle dancing
closer and closer,
reaching out to embrace me.

Drawn inside, I felt
the circles come together,
interlacing and expanding,
as we all danced to a new song
of love and life.

The question "Why me?" often changes to "Where do I belong?" as a person experiences the social consequences of living with cancer. As our culture continues to grow toward disease prevention and wellness, illness becomes more socially unacceptable. Even though people may no longer have rational fears that cancer is contagious, they want to put as much distance as possible between themselves and cancer, and may withdraw from friends who have the disease. This withdrawal comes from a variety of conscious and unconscious sources, such as primitive fears of contact with cancer and confusion about what to say. Thus many people with cancer still experience social ostracism. They may express the feeling of being contaminated or of being perceived by others as contaminated. They still face discrimination from employers and from insurance companies. The psychological dynamics faced by people with cancer, therefore, include shame and rejection. The experience of cancer also includes changes in family roles and relationships. Accepting the limitations and the strengths of relationships may become more challenging during this experience. Anxiety, fear, and anticipatory grief affect the way family members relate to one another as they all live with cancer. The changes taking place in those diagnosed with cancer will naturally affect all those who are in relationship with them. Denial and alienation, as well as increased authenticity and intimacy, are possible consequences.

In spite of the progress made in cancer treatment and the increase in the number of cancer survivors, the word "cancer" still connotes an insidious, destructive force. In fact, one of the definitions of "cancer" is "a pernicious, spreading evil." We hear references to a "cancer destroying our society" or "the cancer in a person's soul." Is it any wonder that people with cancer often feel shame? Some people feel so much shame that they choose to hide their cancer from colleagues at work and even from close friends and family members. A woman with a recent diagnosis of breast cancer came to talk with me before a support group meeting to decide whether or not she wanted to trust this group. She thoroughly quizzed me about the composition of the group, the sponsors of the group, the purpose of the group, and the level of confidentiality. In the group she sat silently until the meeting was almost over. Then she poured out these feelings: "I haven't told anybody except my sister that I have cancer. Not even my mother. I'm afraid to tell my friends at work, because they might avoid me or start talking behind my back or feel uncomfortable around me. I'm really scared that my boss might find out; then she would look at me and my performance in a different light. I feel so ashamed that I got cancer." She went on to tell the group that she had taken great pride in her independence and health. Shaking, she kept repeating, "Now I just feel so ashamed, so ashamed."

Many people find it difficult to interact socially with those who have a life-threatening illness. Such interactions may cause their own fears of illness and mortality to surface, so they choose to avoid acquaintances or abandon friends who have cancer. Even when they are not abandoned, people with cancer often perceive the discomfort of those around them and fear rejection. One young woman said that she could tell by the way people looked at her or by the way people avoided certain topics of conversation whether or not they were aware of her diagnosis. She wondered if some people continued to befriend her simply because they felt sorry for her. She often felt so alienated from her peers that she was unable to interact with them. At times she feared that when people learned the "truth" about her, they would reject her. She expressed her fear that she might lose her job as baby-sitter: "Each time I returned, I wondered whether this would be the time their mother would tell me that I was no longer needed, that she had learned who I really was and was afraid for her sons to be exposed to me."[1]

Even those people who do not avoid being with their friends who have cancer may avoid talking about feelings. They simply cannot understand or do not want to feel the depth of the fear and grief their friends are experiencing. They may remain available for their friends physically but not emotionally. When their friends express painful feelings, they try to cheer them up. Rhonda (see chapters 1, 2, 3,and 4) talked with me about these feelings.

So many friends told me how well I was handling my illness. This put pressure on me to hold up. I felt I couldn't talk openly about my feelings. My roommate wanted me to be upbeat all the time because she believed depression would cause my cancer to recur. I know my friends felt helpless and just wanted to help. But everyone was telling me different things to do—grieve your losses, be positive, smile. It was overwhelming. Sometimes I felt I didn't know which way was up.

The person with cancer is left feeling lonely and confused, maybe even rejected at the deepest level.

Sometimes people with cancer feel isolated not because their friends and families will not talk about feelings, but because each experiences these feelings at different times. Through the period of diagnosis and treatment, most people focus their energies on following the steps prescribed by their physicians and gathering as much information as possible about their illness. They are preoccupied with getting through the rigors of treatment. This task orientation helps them to feel in charge and hopeful. During this time, their friends and families may be feeling the full force of fear and helplessness. After treatment, people with cancer have more time and energy to face the reality of their illness. The big questions concerning life and death surface with accompanying fears of recurrence. At this time, friends and families are breathing a sigh of relief that their loved one has finally finished treatment. They believe their loved one is now well, and they want to put the painful feelings behind them, not understanding that their loved one is only beginning to feel the emotional and spiritual pain of the illness.[2] This difference in timing can cause distress for everyone involved. One young man expressed these feelings.

It's like we're off sync. When I was going through treatment, I could tell how scared my friends were. When they tried to comfort me, I just blew it off or ended up trying to reassure them that I was going to be fine. Now that treatment is over, everyone's telling me they're so glad I'm fine, but I don't feel fine. I feel like I'm going crazy, and I can't tell anyone. They wouldn't understand, and I don't want to make them upset too. They've already been through so much with me.

People with cancer often become emotionally withdrawn from those closest to them because they avoid discussing the illness for fear of upsetting one another or because the fear of loss is too intolerable. In close relationships, such as marriage, the spouses often feel the same degree of anxiety as do the people with cancer. Problems arise not only over differences in timing of partners' feelings but also over their inability to communicate their feelings regarding the illness.[3] A conspiracy of silence develops, as each tries to protect the other's feelings. The wife of a man with an advanced stage of lymphoma talked privately to me about her fear and grief. When I found her husband alone in his room, he confided his fear of dying along with his wish for an end to the pain and struggle. But when they were together in the room, she kept telling him that he was getting better and would soon be able to go back to work. He would respond by smiling and nodding his agreement. Although I tried to facilitate more honest communication, they chose to avoid discussing their painful feelings. As his condition worsened, they seemed to become more distant from each other.

Couples may grow apart because they are coping with different issues. The person with cancer is grappling more directly with spiritual issues of meaning and purpose. He or she is asking the ultimate existential questions concerning life and death. The spouse, on the other hand, is struggling more with the day-to-day stress of balancing caregiving with financial concerns and all the other family responsibilities.[4] Even if they are willing to talk about their feelings, they may have difficulty understanding each other. The result may be feelings of frustration and alienation.

Accepting the limitations of relationships often becomes one of the greatest emotional challenges for people with cancer. Whether or not they want to be more dependent on others, cancer has a way of forcing them to be. They may have to depend on family members and friends for physical as well as emotional and spiritual support. Feeling vulnerable and weak may lead them to expect more from relationships. Even though they may have previously accepted the limitations of a certain relationship, they now want this person to respond with unconditional support and understanding. Lois (see chapter 2) expressed her feelings of disappointment over her mother's inability to give her the support she needed.

My mother has been semi-ill most of her life with various little things, and she's never been a caregiver. Since I've been diagnosed, I've talked with people who know my mother, and they pointed out that she has never changed. The situation changed and that made me change. But she wasn't able to make a change. I guess I was hoping for more. It's a disappointment. It's been a wound that hasn't healed. When I was weak, I felt like she was waiting for my vulnerabilities and attacking me. So I had to cut off communication until I was well enough to deal with it again.

One man talked about his frustration because his wife was not as supportive as he wanted her to be. He said that he finally realized that because he had always been so strong and independent, she had trouble understanding that he needed physical help and emotional support. Although at first he had difficulty asking her for help, he learned to be more direct about his needs.

Tensions often arise in families because of the changes in roles brought by cancer. Roles in marriage relationships may reverse if the illness necessitates resignation from a job or giving up certain domestic chores. Many times the person who becomes ill is the one the family has depended on to keep the family connected physically and emotionally. If someone else in the family does not step into this role, the family may become fragmented. Often parent-child roles are reversed when the parent is ill and the child becomes the primary caregiver. When a young adult is diagnosed with cancer, a parent may have to step back into a caregiving role, thwarting the normal process of relational differentiation that may be taking place or may have been completed. Both parent and child may feel resentment over the forced regression in their relationship.

Mark was diagnosed with acute leukemia when he was twenty years old. After graduation from high school, Mark had chosen to go to a university over a thousand miles from his home because he wanted to be on his own. He lived in a dormitory his first year at the university and in an apartment his second year. When he learned of his diagnosis the summer after his second year, he reluctantly came home for his treatment. His mother and father had been divorced since Mark was five years old. Mark had lived with his mother until he went to college; he had never had a close relationship with his father. Mark moved back into his mother's house and began chemotherapy treatments.

Mark came into the hospital for several extended periods because of infections and other complications from the chemotherapy treatments. His mother, Denise, stayed with him day and night. His father came a few times, but Mark was ambivalent about his presence, and Denise was openly critical of him. Denise believed she should be the one to take care of Mark because she was the only concerned parent. In Mark's presence, she would tell me how much she was sacrificing to care for Mark: she had put her career and her social life on hold. On one rare occasion when Denise was not in the room, Mark told me how he felt about this arrangement.

MARK: Mother's gone to run a few errands. (*sighing*) I wish she would get away more often. She needs to take care of herself.

PASTORAL COUNSELOR: Your mother seems reluctant to leave you.

MARK: I know, and I just wish she would! Don't misunderstand me. I appreciate all she's doing for me, but sometimes I just want to be alone. I know she's scared that something might happen to me, and I'm scared too. And I know I need her right now. But I miss being on my own. She won't even let me do things that I can do for myself. Sometimes she treats me like a baby, and I hate that! I wish she could realize that even though I'm sick, I'm still a grown man. And I don't think her hovering over me all the time is good for me or for her.

P.C.: I'm sure there are so many changes you've had to go through with your illness. But you don't want your mother to treat you like a child.

MARK: It's not that I don't appreciate what she's doing. I guess everybody needs their mother at a time like this, but I wish she would leave me alone more and let me do more for myself. I know she trusts you and likes to talk to you. Maybe you could talk to her about this.

As I observed the interactions between Mark and his mother, it became clear to me that their relationship was not entirely health-inducing. When Denise talked about Mark's condition, she would use the plural, saying things like "We are nauseated today," indicating her enmeshment in the relationship. On the few occasions when I was able to find Denise out of Mark's room, I encouraged her to take better care of herself and to trust Mark and his nurses to take care of him. I also invited her to come to my office to talk more openly about her feelings concerning Mark's illness. She mainly ignored my suggestions and invitations until one day when she was feeling especially anxious and exhausted. In my office, Denise poured out her feelings.

DENISE (*crying and shaking*): I'm so scared that Mark might not make it. He's my baby. I can't bear to think of losing him. It's not that anything new has happened. In fact, the doctor gave us a good report today. Our counts are up, and we're eating better today. We may get to go home soon. I guess it's just that I'm so tired. I've got to be strong for Mark, but sometimes I feel like I'm caving in. I've got to get a grip, because I'm the only reliable person he has. You know how his dad is—we can never depend on him. Sometimes he tells Mark he's coming to see him, and then doesn't even show up. And when he's here, he just sits and watches TV or reads. Mark doesn't feel comfortable asking him to do anything for him. So I've got to be there for Mark all the time. Of course, I want to be, but I'm tired of this. I don't have any life of my own anymore.

P.C.: I can understand how you would be exhausted from taking care of Mark night and day. Have you asked Mark how he feels about your being there all the time?

DENISE: Oh, I know he wants me there. I have a few good friends who have volunteered to stay with Mark, but he wouldn't feel comfortable with them and they wouldn't know what to do for him.

P.C.: Have you asked Mark how he would feel about being by himself more and doing more for himself?

DENISE: I know how much he needs me. I don't think he would get as good care if I weren't there. I know he needs his mother.

P.C.: Denise, you've told me how much your faith means to you and that you know God is helping you through this. What if you thought about God as the Mother who could fill in for you so that you could get some rest. Maybe you don't trust your friends or your ex-husband to take care of Mark, but could you trust Mother God to take care of him?

DENISE: I've never thought of that.

P.C.: There's a passage in the book of Deuteronomy that pictures God as a mother eagle, who stirs up her nest to get the young out on their own. She takes them on her wings and flies with them so that they can learn to fly. Then the mother eagle swoops down to let them fly on their own. But she stays close enough to swoop back under them when they are too weary and weak to fly on their own. Mark had been out there flying on his own for a few years; then he became ill and needed motherly care again. You have been giving him that care, but you don't have to do it alone. Our Divine Mother Eagle will also help you when you are too weak and weary to fly alone. Can you trust Mother God to give you some relief and to take care of Mark?

DENISE (*crying*): Maybe I could. I'd like to. That's a beautiful story and a comforting way to think of God.

Pastoral interventions that include freeing and comforting sacred images help to heal the dysfunction in relationships caused by cancer. The image of God as Mother can serve to relieve human mothers of feelings of overresponsibility for their children with cancer. In addition, the Mother Eagle pictures a healthy differentiation in the mother-child relationship. As Denise and I continued to explore these images in pastoral counseling, she gradually began to spend time away from Mark, giving him more freedom to take care of himself. This pastoral intervention resulted in benefits for both Denise and Mark.[5]

Sacred stories, along with sacred images, are among the pastoral interventions that may guide people with cancer back into the circle of healthy relationship. People who place authority in biblical stories may find help in connecting these stories and their own stories. As they identify with characters in the biblical stories, their feelings of isolation decrease as their energy for reaching out to others in similar circumstances increases.

Jean, a single woman in her forties, came for pastoral counseling several months after she was diagnosed with ovarian cancer. A successful accountant, Jean valued her independent lifestyle. Since she did not have a close relationship with her parents or siblings, she had chosen to live a long distance from them. Jean's closest relationships were with friends at work and in her Jewish congregation, of which she had been an active member for many years. Her friends had been supportive through her surgery and were continuing to offer support as she was now having chemotherapy treatments. While Jean appreciated their encouragement, it often made her feel lonely. She felt that she could not tell them how she really felt, because they were trying so hard to cheer her up.

JEAN: Sometimes I feel like I'm going crazy. Everyone's telling me I look fine, and they know I'm going to be fine, but that's not how I feel. I haven't lost my hair yet or had any other visible changes and I keep going to work and doing everything I've always done, so they think I'm doing great. They tell me how impressed they are by the way I'm dealing with this. They just don't know. I'm going to the same places and doing the same things, but nothing's the same anymore.

I go to work, and it's like going into a foreign country. Nothing seems familiar anymore; everything feels incongruent. That's why I feel like I'm going crazy. Everybody thinks I'm the same, but I'm just going through the motions. Nobody can understand this.

PASTORAL COUNSELOR: What do you think would happen if you told your close friends what's really going on inside you?

JEAN: They might not be able to handle it. There's no way they can understand. It might scare them too much to hear how terrified I am.

P.C.: Then what would they do?

JEAN: They wouldn't stick around. They might want to, but they couldn't, because they wouldn't know what to do. It would all be too frightening for them.

P.C.: Jean, do you remember the biblical story of Ruth and Naomi?

JEAN: Yes, but what does that have to do with anything?

P.C.: It occurs to me that you may feel like Naomi and may need someone like Ruth. You remember that Naomi suffered many losses. First, she lost her husband, and then she lost her two sons. In that time and society, women were defined mainly through their relationships with men. So Naomi felt that everything had changed in her life. She decided to go back to her homeland of Judah, which she had left many years before. But she knew this land would not feel the same because so much had changed in her life. She said that she had left her country "full" and now she was returning "empty." Like you, she was going back to a familiar place, but nothing would be the same. Ruth, her daughter-in-law, had also lost a husband, and she had no children. Because she could understand Naomi's feelings of emptiness, Ruth left her country of Moab to go with Naomi to Judah. Together they would go to seek a new life. Do you have someone, like Ruth, who will go with you into another land to a new life? Someone who's going through an experience similar to yours?

JEAN (*crying*): None of my close friends have had cancer, so they can't understand what I'm going through.

P.C.: How would you feel about coming to a support group where you could get to know others who are experiencing cancer?

JEAN: That would probably help. Maybe there would be some people who understand my feelings. Maybe I could find someone who would be like Ruth to me.

P.C.: I believe you would find people in the group who could understand what you're going through. You would find a person or a circle of people who could be Ruth to you.

People living with cancer draw hope from many sources. When they have supportive family and friends, they find hope through these relationships. But sometimes the manner of expression and the timing of the hope offered by loved ones leaves the person with cancer feeling misunderstood and lonely. By walking with that person and hearing future stories of despair as well as hope, pastoral counselors may aid the hoping process. Jean's future story that her friends would reject and abandon her if they knew her true feelings made her feel isolated and despairing. Imagining a future story in which she was encircled by people who understood her feelings brought her hope. By opening the possibility of a such a future story, I was hoping with Jean and allowing her to "borrow hope" from me.[6] Jean did begin coming to a support group. After several sessions, she expressed relief and gratitude that she had found a place where she could express her honest feelings and new friends who could go with her on her cancer journey.

One of the most effective pastoral interventions with people experiencing cancer is connecting them with others going through similar experiences. As they identify with the stories of others, they begin the journey toward healing from isolation and alienation. A turning point often occurs when a person with cancer comes to the recognition, "I am not alone." Mutual relationships in which people feel heard, seen, understood, and known are vital to a person's spiritual, emotional, and physical well-being.

Psychiatrist David Spiegel set out to examine what he believed were "overstated claims" of the relationship between the body and mind. In a research study of eighty-six women with metastatic breast cancer, he sought to prove that psychosocial support groups could improve the quality of life without affecting its quantity (length). In the groups, the women discussed their fears about dying, ways of living the remainder of their lives as richly as possible, strengthening family relationships, improving doctor-patient communication, building a strong sense of mutual support, and controlling pain and other somatic symptoms. Spiegel reported that the women developed close bonds with one another and came to feel socially integrated. They felt a sense of belonging and acceptance through sharing a common dilemma. The groups countered the social alienation that often divides people with cancer from their well-meaning friends and family who cannot fully understand them. To Spiegel's surprise, he discovered that the women in the support groups increased not only their quality of life but also the length of their lives. They lived twice as long as the women not in the groups. Spiegel concluded that social relationships affect survival, and thus comprehensive cancer treatment should involve intensive psychosocial support, along with medical treatments.[7]

In her research, psychologist Lauren K. Ayers likewise discovered that social support, involving a sense of belonging and participation with others, was among the psychological factors that affect the course of breast cancer. She concluded that community is central to healthy psychological and physical functioning.[8] David K. Wellisch states that cancer support groups may increase in their importance by helping to fill the service gaps left by diminishing health care resources, including mental health resources.[9] Research provides empirical evidence for the efficacy of community, which people of faith have long acknowledged. As spiritual guides, pastoral counselors have a unique opportunity to help people experience the sacred power of community.

For many months I encouraged Lena to come to a cancer support group. Estranged from her family, she had chosen to live alone. She had many business associates and a few close friends. After her cancer diagnosis, one of her friends began to withdraw from Lena. The growing distance in their relationship confused and hurt Lena. During this time, she also realized that her relationship with another friend was not reciprocal. This friend had always taken more than she had given to Lena, and now that Lena had cancer, she did not know how to help. While Lena was in the hospital after surgery, this friend called and talked about her own problems instead of listening to Lena's concerns. Because of some negative experiences growing up in church, Lena had not been involved in a religious community for many years. Finally, she followed my recommendation and came to a weekly cancer support group.

For the first four weeks, Lena sat quietly in the group and left immediately after the session concluded, without interacting with other group members. In the fifth session she began to talk about her feelings of loneliness and fear. Others in the group identified with Lena and encouraged her to tell her story. The group's empathetic response seemed to enliven her, and she stayed after the group to socialize with people. The next week Lena was one of the most active participants, both giving and receiving support. The focus of the seventh session was on spiritual issues raised by a cancer diagnosis. As we were discussing ways the cancer experience affected participants' images of God, Lena began to cry. She told the group that her church had given her the idea of God as a demanding, punitive parent. She had finally rejected that image of God, but had not found anything to replace it. She said, "Here I've experienced love and acceptance like I've never known before. Isn't that what God's supposed to be like? Now when I think of God, I think of all of you in this group. I feel God through you." I affirmed her picture of God as this community in which she felt deep understanding and love.

In the Christian tradition, the metaphor of the body of Christ conveys this notion of divine reality mediated through many members of one community. Vital to the Jewish tradition is the community of faith in covenant relationship with God and with one another; this community brings life and hope. Pastoral counselors can use the image of God as Community to guide people with cancer to develop empathic relationships that lead to feelings of self-acceptance and divine-acceptance. Bonds developed in cancer support groups also increase the hoping capacity in participants. Support communities are a form of ritual experience based on shared stories and feelings.[10] Formal rituals led by pastoral facilitators can also help communities of people with cancer discover meaning and deepen relationships. (See Appendix A for an example of such a ritual.)

One of the most powerful sources of hope for people with cancer may be the presence and story of a cancer survivor. Newly diagnosed with an aggressive form of lymphoma, Stan faced a grueling regimen of high-dose chemotherapy and then a marrow transplantation. Stan approached his treatment with a stoic attitude, believing that he was to be "strong" for his family. Being "strong" to Stan meant hiding his feelings from everyone. His family and friends interpreted his demeanor as his having no problem dealing with his cancer, and they praised him for his positive attitude. As Stan was preparing to begin treatment, his physician noticed that Stan looked depressed. Stan admitted that he was a little "down," and the physician recommended a support group. At the first group meeting Stan heard the story of one of the volunteer leaders who had gone through a marrow transplant six years before in treatment of lymphoma. Stan expressed surprise and delight after hearing this story. He said to the volunteer, "I didn't want to let on, but I came in here feeling really down and scared. I don't know anyone with cancer, and I wasn't sure what I'd see. But your story gives me great encouragement. In fact, you are living, walking, breathing hope to me!" Another long-term cancer survivor in the group responded, "The hope I received from other survivors in support groups has been my salvation! I know the groups have been my emotional salvation, and I believe they contribute in some way to my physical health."

By helping people with cancer connect with one another either individually or in groups, pastoral counselors participate in their movement from alienation to increased authenticity in relationships. In cancer support groups or in one-on-one encounters with another person with cancer, people often find themselves telling their life stories more openly and honestly than ever before. This open style of communication may carry over into other relationships. As one man said in a support group, "I don't want to waste any more time trying to impress people or worrying about what they think about me. Now I'm going to be myself and say how I truly feel, and if they don't like it, that's too bad." Many people feel such relief from the level of honesty they experience in support groups that they develop greater authenticity in their other relationships as well. One woman talked about her newfound boldness: "This group has made me bolder about expressing my own needs and feelings. I used not to be very assertive when it came to my own needs, but now I just say, 'This is the way it is, and this is what I've got to have.'"

Through authentic relationships with others experiencing cancer, many people grow toward greater mutuality in all their relationships. Within support groups Lena developed healthy relationships based on reciprocity; she was gradually able to extend this experience to her relationships with family and friends. Another woman developed a mutual relationship with her husband as a result of her experience with cancer and of her experiences in cancer support groups. She said, "My relationship with my husband has become more equal. I used to do almost everything, and he let me do it all. I told him I can't do everything I used to do around the house and keep the books. He's learned some new skills, and now we divide chores more equally." When mutuality in relationships increases, there is the potential for greater intimacy.

In one research study, 65 percent of the spouses of people with cancer reported increased intimacy in the marriage after the cancer diagnosis. People with cancer and their spouses stated that the most important factor in their quality of life was their personal relationships.[11] Intimate, loving relationships have powerful healing potential. Larry Dossey asserts that love "alleviates pain and suffering, and it sometimes sets the stage for physical improvement or cure." But he goes on to describe an even greater benefit of loving relationships: "Love unmasks the illusion of isolation. It subsumes (but does not eradicate) individuality by making possible the experience of a collective, unitary consciousness . . . love reveals our hidden identity by showing us that in some sense we are infinite, eternal, immortal, and one."[12]

In our most intimate relationships, we catch a glimpse of Ultimate Reality as Being in Relationship. For this reason, disruptions in close relationships that often come with cancer can shake people at their core. As people struggle with the social consequences of cancer, they walk along a difficult path filled with danger and possibility. Sometimes they feel overwhelmed by feelings of shame and fear of rejection. Often they feel that those closest to them deny their feelings or simply cannot understand them. Changes in their roles within their families may leave them wondering where they belong. Feelings of alienation may take them to the point of despair. Pastoral counselors have the holy opportunity of walking with people through confusion and isolation to authenticity and intimacy in relationships. Pastoral interventions that include images of God as empathic, mutual Community empower people to develop health-enhancing relationships. If we suggest and explore many divine images of nurturing and healing in our pastoral relationships with people, we may guide them toward dynamic, multidimensional spiritual experiences that extend to their relationships with family and friends. By helping them connect their stories with biblical stories and with the stories of others going through the cancer experience, pastoral guides help them to discover the sacred value and the healing possibilities of their own stories. Hope then replaces despair as relationships deepen and expand toward a future of loving connection.

Chapter Seven

Who Am I Now?
Embodiment
and Sexuality

A reflection in the mirror
staring at me, glaring at me,
pierces my being
with fears of non-being.
Who is this? Who am I?

I am in a different image,
not the bald and scarred
one staring back at me.
Where is the image of the
One in whose image I was created?

The reflection keeps looking at me,
never leaving nor forsaking me, crying as I cry.
Could it be that the image whom
I reflect also reflects me,
even in my imperfection?

As cancer and its treatments bring changes to a person's body, questions of identity naturally arise. Since body, mind, and spirit are one, physical changes affect a person's whole being. Cancer can wreak havoc on a person's body. Treatment regimens may significantly change a person's physical appearance and sexual functioning. Fluctuations in weight, loss of hair, and decrease in sexual desire are common, although usually temporary, side effects of chemotherapy. Changes in color and texture of skin are common side effects of radiation therapy. Skin rashes may cover the entire body as a result of graft versus host disease following marrow transplantation. Disfiguring surgeries frequently affect embodiment as it relates to sexuality. Loss of ovaries, uterus, breasts, or testicles can affect a person's sexual identity and sexual functioning. Cancer treatment can affect the reproductive system, leaving a person infertile. Colon cancer often results in a colostomy that may adversely affect body image and sexual identity. In addition to the myriad changes that may accompany treatment, the cancer itself may cause weight loss, bloating, skin discoloration, infertility, and other bodily changes. In the midst of aggressive treatment of her leukemia, a forty-year-old woman lamented, "When I look in the mirror, I don't see myself anymore."

The physical changes that accompany cancer and its treatment challenge a person's self-esteem and identity. Accepting an altered body image may be extremely difficult. Feeling less attractive may cause people to feel less lovable and thus to fear social and sexual rejection. They may suffer distress from knowing they no longer look the way they want to look.[1] Integrating the changes in body image into their overall self-concept takes time and energy. Treatments for prostate, gynecological, breast, and colon-rectal cancers especially threaten a person's physical and sexual image.

Men with prostate cancer must cope not only with the loss of control and the loss of feelings of invulnerability that come with any cancer, but also with the possible loss of a part of their sexuality. These losses may severely threaten gender identity. One man lamented, "My cancer took my manhood away." Another commented, "If I can't have sex, I might as well be dead."[2] A prostatectomy, one of the most common treatments for prostate cancer, may leave a man impotent and incontinent. This surgery may result in impotence from either physical damage to the nerves or from emotional trauma that interferes with sexual arousal. Other treatments for prostate cancer may cause problems with sexual functioning: radiation poses some risk of permanent impotence; chemotherapy and hormone therapy may decrease sexual drive. Any man with prostate cancer is likely to experience performance anxiety to the degree that he will experience temporary or intermittent impotence. For some men, the loss of bladder control poses a greater threat to their identity. They may feel reduced to the status of infants. This loss of control may become a constant reminder of the overall feelings of loss of control they are experiencing. In our culture in which men have been socialized to exercise a high degree of control and to place great importance on sexual performance, the losses sustained from prostate cancer may lead to questions concerning their manhood.[3]

Testicular cancer, usually occurring in young men, likewise presents challenges to sexuality. Common treatments for this type of cancer are surgery, chemotherapy, and radiation, all of which can interfere with sexual functioning. After surgery, these men often experience a decrease in sexual satisfaction and in the frequency of sexual intercourse. Chemotherapy and radiation often cause even greater problems in sexual functioning. Chemotherapy may deplete men of their energy and desire for sex. Treatments for testicular cancer may also result in temporary or permanent sterility. For this reason, physicians usually counsel men to store their sperm before beginning treatment. After surgery, some men feel less attractive and choose to have a testicular prosthesis. A research study of the effects of testicular cancer on sexual functioning in married couples revealed disparities between husbands' and wives' perceptions of sexual problems. The husbands perceived greater long-term problems in sexual function than did their wives, who felt that the illness had increased intimacy.[4]

Women treated for uterine, ovarian, cervical, and other gynecological cancers may struggle with their feminine identity. Since the organs affected are associated with sexuality, as well as with childbearing, women may feel a threat to their femininity. After a hysterectomy, one woman remarked, "Now I feel like an empty shell." Another said that she no longer felt "like a real woman." Some women fear that gynecological surgery will damage their ability to have orgasms. While a hysterectomy does not cause physical changes that would prevent a woman from having an orgasm, it may cause emotional changes that diminish her sexual desire. Anxiety about her femininity, fear of rejection, and lowered self-esteem are among the emotions that may decrease sexual drive. Women who have had a vulvectomy may have problems reaching orgasm and may experience distress over the physical disfigurement of this surgery. Although a hysterectomy leaves no visible disfigurement, it often leaves deep emotional wounds. Whether or not a woman grieves the loss of her childbearing capacity after a hysterectomy, she often feels a void. Sometimes her feelings are complicated because those closest to her cannot see her loss and cannot understand its importance to her identity as a woman.

Treatment for breast cancer often brings visible physical changes that affect a woman's self-esteem. In our culture, breasts are a major symbol of female sexuality and beauty. Thus many women feel that they are no longer sexually attractive following a mastectomy, and they go through a sexual identity crisis.[5] One woman said that the loss of a breast had made her feel "abnormal, deformed, and freakish." Another refused the recommended breast surgery, saying, "I'd rather die a whole person than live without a breast." A woman of any age may experience mastectomy as a disfigurement that profoundly affects her sense of self. Both physical and emotional changes that come with mastectomy, as well as with chemotherapy and other treatments for breast cancer, may cause changes in sexual desire and functioning. The feelings of the woman and her partner about her appearance after the loss of a breast or breasts influence their sexual relationship. Reconstructive surgery offers psychological benefits to many women, increasing their feelings of wholeness and their sexual satisfaction.[6] One woman describes this surgery as "being put back together again." Although reconstruction may leave the woman with breasts as attractive or more attractive than before her mastectomy, she will still grieve the loss of her original breasts. No matter how beautiful her reconstructed breasts are, they are not her original breasts, and they do not have the same sexual feelings.

Treatment for cancers of the colon and/or rectum may result in significant physical changes that affect body image and self-esteem. Many people find the idea of having a colostomy to be repulsive, fearing it more than cancer. One man said that his colostomy made him "feel dirty all the time." A woman commented, "I feel like everyone can see and smell this bag." Some people withdraw from social interaction because of the shame and embarrassment they feel. They feel disgusted with their own bodies and believe that others will also be disgusted and reject them. Others avoid social situations because of the practical problem of finding facilities to dispose of dressings and bags. People may experience sexual difficulties from damage to the pelvic nerves during surgery or from distaste and embarrassment felt by themselves or their partners.[7] One man expressed the fear that the bag on his abdomen might leak during sexual intercourse and that his wife would find him "unclean and undesirable." Although our society's attitudes toward discussions of bodily functions is changing, some people still have difficulty talking about their struggles with colostomies and sexuality. Their self-esteem then suffers further from their feelings of loneliness and isolation.

Experience with any type of cancer can shatter people's trust in their bodies and diminish their capacity to enjoy their bodies. In our culture cancer is still so strongly associated with dread, horror, uncleanness, and sometimes even contagion that it can have a devastating impact on people's feelings of being in their own bodies. Their bodies may feel like battlefields that threaten to destroy them instead of playgrounds that bring them pleasure.[8] One woman expressed these feelings, "My body has betrayed me, and now I can't trust it anymore. Sometimes I feel angry toward my body and want to disconnect from it." Since they have associated their bodies with illness, discomfort, and distress, it may be difficult to recapture feelings of wholeness, pleasure, and aliveness.

Loss of fertility as a result of some types of cancer treatments may have adverse effects on a person's body image and self-worth. Surgery, chemotherapy, radiation, and hormone therapy can leave people with temporary or permanent infertility. Learning they are permanently sterile may come as a shocking blow to survivors of childhood cancer who were not told or did not understand that their cancer treatment would destroy their capacity for biological parenthood. Even when they do understand the possible consequences of treatment, their main concern initially is their own survival. After surviving treatment, the reality of the loss of fertility may come as an overwhelming blow. This loss may lead to anger and resentment in a marriage relationship or fear of rejection in a single person. Single people often describe infertility as a major obstacle in dating, as they worry about when and how to tell the other person about not only the cancer but also the resulting sterility. They may see themselves as biological failures and therefore undesirable to the opposite sex. People suffer differing degrees of grief from the loss of fertility, depending upon their goals and the degree to which their identity involves biological parenting. One woman describes her feelings of loss, "I've lost a part of me, a part of my future."[9] For many people infertility comes as a cruel double betrayal by their bodies; not only has the cancer in their bodies made their own survival tenuous, but also their bodies will not cooperate in extending themselves into the future through children.

Cancer and its treatment result in many physical changes and accompanying feelings of loss. The degree and permanence of these changes, as well as the importance of body image to a person's identity, influence his or her response. Pastoral counselors must examine the impact of the disease on each person's body image and self-esteem.

Tonya, a married woman in her twenties, came for pastoral counseling several weeks before she was to have a hysterectomy to treat ovarian cancer. In our first session she poured out her story. Tonya's alcoholic father had been physically and emotionally abusive to her mother and to her two older brothers. Her father and one of her brothers had sexually abused Tonya. Her father left the family when Tonya was eight years old. Her mother, struggling for the family's financial survival, was emotionally distant. Tonya never told her mother about the sexual abuse she had suffered. When Tonya was in high school, she became sexually active. She believed that the main way she could receive the affection and approval she craved was through sex. Her mother took Tonya and her brothers to a conservative Christian church, where she learned that her sexual promiscuity was sinful. Throughout her teenage years she struggled with the tension between her longing for affection and her fear of punishment for her sexual behavior. Now in her twenties, she was changing her lifestyle. Working her way through college made her feel good about herself, and she was now feeling some fulfillment through her vocation of teaching, as well as through her leadership roles in her church. She had been married for two years, and described her marriage as "reasonably good." She concluded her story, however, by telling me that she believed that she had caused her cancer, that it was "punishment" for her "past sins."

In our second session, Tonya expressed grief over her loss of a "normal" life. She pondered the question, "What is a normal life?" She felt that her life had always been filled with obstacles, and that she was tired of this kind of life. She was trying so hard to create a different kind of life for herself. As a part of facilitating her grief, I tried to help her get in touch with her anger over losses in her past as well as the losses she now faced with her cancer diagnosis. I suggested that her past story indicated sins against her. Although she continued to express her belief that her cancer was related to her promiscuous sex life, she moved in the direction of recognizing the part others had played in her lifestyle. She had internalized the erroneous message that the way for her to receive approval was through her body's sexual capacity.

In our third session, several days before her hysterectomy, Tonya dealt more directly with her fears and grief concerning the surgery.

TONYA: I'm terrified about the surgery—not so much the surgery itself, but what it might do to me, how I'll be afterward.

PASTORAL COUNSELOR: How do you see your future after the surgery?

TONYA (*crying*): I don't know who I'll be anymore. I was wanting so badly to have a normal life, and now I can't. I know I won't be able to have children. The doctor's already told me that, because she'll have to take my uterus and ovaries. That was a big goal for me. I wanted to have a normal family. And now that's about to be taken away. (*crying*) I don't know how my husband's going to feel about me now.

P.C.: You're really hurting from the losses you're anticipating.

TONYA (*crying*): Having children is really important to me. I know I can adopt, but that just doesn't feel the same. I wanted the experience of giving birth to my own child from my own body.

P.C.: Giving birth was an important part of your picture of yourself in the future.

TONYA: It's just so hard to give that up. I know I haven't lost everything. I love my job, and I guess my husband will still love me, even though I can't have children.

P.C.: Have you and your husband talked about your feelings?

TONYA: Not really. He never expresses his feelings very much, and I'm too afraid to ask him how he feels. He doesn't know about my past. He'd probably think I caused this cancer too. I hope he'll love me even though my body won't be normal anymore, and I can't have children. He really wanted children too.

P.C.: You're hoping that he will love you for more than your body's ability to have children. Tonya, do you remember the story about Jesus and a woman who praised his teaching? Jesus was healing and teaching in a large crowd of people, and a woman called out to him, "Blessed is the womb that bore you and the breasts that nursed you!" This woman had thoroughly internalized the prejudices of her society that reduced women to wombs and breasts, so she believed that she was giving a high compliment to Jesus and to his mother. Rejecting this image of women, Jesus replied, "Blessed rather are those who hear the word of God and obey it!" (Luke 11:27–28). Jesus' reply to the woman indicates that spiritual and intellectual capacities are most important for everyone, and that it is our relationship to God that makes us blessed, not our childbearing capacity.

TONYA: I hope my husband will have that kind of attitude. I've always felt that guys loved me mainly for my body and what it could do for them. But that story reminds me that God sees me as more, and I need to see myself as more.

P.C.: The story you told me about your past shows that you've already made many healthy changes in your life. My hope is that you will continue to grow in loving yourself for who you are as a whole person.

This pastoral conversation illustrates the use of story to facilitate change in a person's thinking about embodiment and sexuality. In this encounter with Tonya and in my ministry with others struggling with embodiment issues through their cancer experience, I feel the tension and paradox of my theology of the unity of body, mind, and spirit. Persons with cancer experience all of life through their bodies, marked by losses and changes; however, they are more than their diseased bodies. Sometimes they may feel they are no more than the labels they often hear given to themselves in hospitals, such as "non-Hodgkin's lymphoma patients." Our pastoral role is to remind them of their whole personhood. When we focus on the mind and spirit, we walk a fine line in order to keep from splitting mind and spirit from body. Recognition that physical losses and changes are intricately connected to identity will help us facilitate people's expressions of fear and grief. At the same time our belief that their bodies are not the sum total of their personhood enables us to offer hope.

Sacred images also help in the movement toward hope and wholeness when body image has been altered by the cancer experience. The way people envision deity influences the way they see themselves and feel about themselves when their bodies undergo change and loss. An image of God as perfect and unchanging may cause people experiencing cancer to feel far removed from God as their bodies suffer many changes and their physical imperfections increase. Images of a God who suffers along with humanity hold potential for bringing comfort to those with cancer. The images of Lover and Wounded Healer offer creative possibilities.

Sally McFague illuminates the image of God as Lover, demonstrating the important implications of this image for healing. The image of Lover emphasizes the importance of the physical body, undercutting the body-spirit split in traditional views of redemption. God as Lover works actively to bring well-being to the beloved, as healer of the division in the body and liberator of the oppressed. McFague parallels the work of Lover with Jesus' ministry of healing the sick and liberating the oppressed. God as Lover brings healing through identification with sufferers in their pain. There are no lovers who do not feel wounded and no liberators who do not experience oppression. Solidarity with the sufferings of the beloved is essential to the kind of love implicit in the model of God as Lover.[10]

When Charles (see chapters 1, 2, and 3) was first diagnosed with Hodgkin's disease, he was single. After a year of chemotherapy and radiation, followed by surgery, Charles thought he was cured. During this time he became engaged to a young woman he had been dating for several years. A few months later he learned that his cancer had recurred. Charles and the young woman stayed together as he went through another year of treatment, but the cancer took its toll on their relationship. Even though he had banked his sperm so that he could possibly father their children and did everything else he could to assure her that they could have a normal married life, her fears led her to withdraw from the relationship. This rejection magnified his feelings about the changes cancer had brought to his body. He describes going through a period of "depression and self-loathing." His weight gain from the medication he was taking increased these feelings. When his hair fell out, he thought, "O God, here I am this fat, bald guy!"

Through this time in which his self-esteem was threatened by changes in his body image and feelings of rejection, the image of God as absolute, unconditional Love brought him healing and hope. He says that getting in touch with Love made him regain a feeling of wholeness. Charles associates this kind of Love with Jesus, who also suffered physically and emotionally. The image of incarnate, suffering Love helped Charles to feel understood and loved no matter how he looked.

A year later Charles became engaged to another young woman, Donna. Several months before the wedding was scheduled, he talked with me concerning some of his anxieties. He had just found out that he had to go through another round of chemotherapy treatment. He expressed some fears that chemotherapy would affect his sexual functioning. He was also concerned about the weight he would gain through treatment and about the inevitable loss of hair. I also wondered if Charles feared that Donna might leave him as his former fiancee had done.

CHARLES: I know I'll get fat again, but I really don't care so much now. And I'm sure I'll lose my hair. That causes me some anxiety. I tried to talk my oncologist into waiting until after the wedding to start the treatments, but he convinced me that I have to go ahead and have at least a few treatments. Donna and I have already had our wedding pictures made, so we could be sure I'd have hair in them—and not be too fat. Maybe my hair won't start falling out until after the wedding.

PASTORAL COUNSELOR: It's hard to think about going through these physical changes at this important time in your life. What does Donna think about all this?

CHARLES: With Donna, it's really not been an issue. I just know that she doesn't love me for the way I look. To have that confidence is awesome. She helps convince me that my hair has nothing to do with who I am. I like it when it looks good, and I like to be good-looking, but that really has very little to do with me. When I lose my hair and I get so fat that my clothes don't fit, it'll bother me, but not so much now. My relationship with Donna has taken my confidence to a new level because I never thought someone as great as she is would ever really like me, especially after all I've gone through. I really feel good about myself now.

P.C.: It sounds to me that Donna has embodied for you the image of unconditional Love you have described to me as bringing you healing. Like this Divine Lover, she loves you no matter how you look. She loves you for who you are as a whole person. And even though she hasn't been through cancer, perhaps she's been through changes and losses that help her identify with you.

CHARLES: You're right. She understands me and totally accepts me no matter what, so I know she won't leave me.

The sacred image of Lover helped relieve Charles's anxieties as he looked forward to his wedding. He felt reassured that the love and understanding he experienced from Donna was like that he had experienced from the Divine Lover. Now he felt confident that Donna would not leave him, no matter what changes his body went through as a result of his cancer treatment. The wedding took place as scheduled. As Charles had feared, he lost his hair before the wedding. He told me later, "I got married bald! But it really wasn't an issue."

Coming from Henri Nouwen's model of the human minister as a "wounded healer," the image of a divine Wounded Healer may be comforting and empowering to those who suffer significant bodily changes as a result of cancer. Nouwen says that when we as human beings realize that "we do not have to escape our pains, but that we can mobilize them into a common search for life, those very pains are transformed from expressions of despair into signs of hope."[11] The image of deity as one who does not escape pain, but who suffers woundedness along with us, brings Divine Presence and Power closer to us. This image of Wounded Healer is similar to McFague's model of God as Lover, who is in solidarity with the sufferings of the beloved. The image of Wounded Healer may be more accessible than the image of Lover to those persons with cancer who have had painful experiences with human lovers.

In addition, the Wounded Healer may evoke nonhuman, as well as human, sacred images. Increasingly, people with cancer are raising questions about possible environmental causes of their disease. They wonder if the pollution in the air and water has contributed to their cancer. Although there are no simple, definitive answers to these questions at this time, they raise the possibility of imaging the Wounded Healer as the earth. Matthew Fox revisions the paschal mystery as Mother Earth crucified and dying, but rising again with new healing power as human beings reconnect with Earth. Fox states that this new symbol of Jesus as Mother Earth crucified yet rising holds power to awaken us to the survival of Earth and to our own best selves. Mother Earth is wounded and weeping, but holds potential to bring blessing and healing as we reestablish a holy relationship with Mother Earth.[12] Howard Clinebell likewise writes about Earth as deeply wounded, but as offering hopeful possibilities for healing. He proposes a therapeutic model called "ecotherapy," which involves a reciprocal process of healing ourselves as we heal Mother-Father Earth. Ecotherapy includes stories of nature's healing power, encouraging people to find nurture in nature to reduce stress and heal grief and in the use of earth rituals. Listening to the anguished cries of the wounded earth can contribute to our own healing as well as the healing of the earth.[13]

A year after having a radical hysterectomy in treatment of cervical cancer, Catherine came for pastoral counseling. For the past year her energy had been consumed by visits to physicians, tests, surgery, and radiation treatments. As is common with those experiencing cancer, it was not until after Catherine had completed all her treatments that she began to grieve her losses. A single woman who had recently had her thirtieth birthday, Catherine was close to despair as she talked to me about her future story.

CATHERINE: I probably won't ever get married now. It's too scary to think about bringing up my surgery and my cancer when I date. I just can't imagine how I will be in a love relationship now. First, I would have to think of a way to tell him I had cancer. That would probably be enough to scare him off. Then I'd have to tell him I can't have children. I have too much going against me now. I've always dreamed of having a family—husband and children. I've got to give that up. (*crying*) My body feels too damaged now.

PASTORAL COUNSELOR: You're grieving many losses.

CATHERINE: I really do want a relationship. But whoever I get involved with will not have gone through all this with me, so how can he really understand me? But I've just got to get on with my life. I'm sick and tired of cancer and letting cancer rule my life. So I have to get out there and find somebody, whether he understands or not. It may not be what I'd wanted, but I've got to have something in my life besides cancer.

P.C.: Catherine, I believe you could have more hope about finding a meaningful relationship if you would let yourself grieve your losses first.

CATHERINE (*crying*): I know you're right. But I don't seem to be able to do that. It's just too painful to stop and think about it.

P.C.: One time when I was suffering from a very painful loss, I tried to do the same thing you're doing—avoid thinking about it, hoping it would just go away. But, of course, it didn't. Finally one day when my heart felt so heavy I could hardly breathe, I decided to take a long walk in the woods. It was fall, and the trees flamed with shades of gold and red. Trees have always brought me feelings of peace and nurture, and now I realize that it's because I grew up in Louisiana among pine, oak, and magnolia trees. That day as I was walking and crying out my grief, I heard a stream making gurgling sounds. Coming closer, I saw a dingy brown film over the water and scraps of paper and other trash in the stream. I sat down beside the stream and let my sobs come freely. Somehow I felt the stream had also suffered wounds and understood my grief and was crying with me. For many weeks, I went back to walk in that place, to let the trees and the stream bring me healing as I continued to work through my grief. I wonder if you could find a place in nature to go where you could be nurtured and comforted as you grieve. Sometimes through nature I imagine the Creator as a Wounded Healer.

CATHERINE: Your story reminds me of times when I've gone to the mountains to relieve stress and painful memories. Maybe that's because I grew up in Colorado. I guess I either need to go back there for a little while or find some place around here where I can let out my feelings.

Catherine decided to take a two-week vacation and go to Colorado. When she came back to see me after her return, she looked rested, and she talked much more hopefully about her future. She was still grieving the loss of her capacity for biological birthing, but she spoke of other ways that she saw herself giving birth in the future. As the mountains near her home in Colorado had survived in spite of pollution and continued to bring healing through their beauty, perhaps she could bring healing out of her pain. She had begun to write about her feelings with the hope of publishing a book and speaking to groups about her cancer experience. She also expressed more hope about finding a meaningful relationship and having a family, perhaps adopting children.

Mildred, a forty-five-year-old married woman, made the decision not to have reconstructive surgery following her mastectomy. After a year of treatment for her breast cancer, including high-dose chemotherapy and radiation along with her surgery, she wanted nothing else done to her body. Mildred, an attractive woman always immaculately groomed, described herself as a perfectionist. She expressed her feelings that her body had suffered abuse through all the treatment she had undergone. She said that the loss of her breast had not affected her body image "that much," and it had not changed her relationship with her husband. Her husband, focused mainly on her survival, was glad that the breast was gone because it contained the cancer. The loss of her hair, however, presented some challenge for her self-esteem. She felt that her thick auburn hair had been one of her best features. But what troubled her most about her body image was her posture. One day when she was walking in a shopping mall, she caught a glimpse of her image in a store window. She expressed disbelief at what she saw: "There I was walking along like a little old lady. I couldn't believe it! I don't know where that came from. It still haunts me. I was wondering why I was slumping so badly, and then I thought that maybe I'm protecting my chest because it's still sensitive or I'm self-conscious about it."

As Mildred worked through many grief issues in our counseling sessions, she continued to express concern about changes in her body. She was trying hard to improve her posture, but she wondered if her body would ever be the same. In my efforts to help her move toward feelings of wholeness in spite of her physical changes, I remembered her positive response to a presentation I had made in a support group in which I had circulated some visual images of God created by the artist Doris Klein. I invited her to look through these again to see if any of them spoke to her experience of pain at this time. She looked at several and then focused on one called "The Torn Woman." This picture depicts a tall woman with a steadfast countenance walking forward; the earth forms the background of the picture. A chasm runs through the center of the woman and the earth. Mildred turned the card over and read Doris Klein's comments on the image: "The figure embodies not only her own woundedness, but the wounds of all women, children and men—the wounds of the earth herself. Not diminished by the pain, the torn woman, with head held high, strides forward with determination, moving with hope into the light."[14] Mildred turned the card back over and looked intently at the image. "I'm like this woman," she said. "My body has this wound that will always be there, but I'm strong and determined like she is. She's not perfect, but she stands tall, and so can I."

As she continued to heal, I suggested that Mildred take walks in a place that she found beautiful and comforting. She told me that on one of these walks she saw a magnificent tree that reminded her of "The Torn Woman." The tree stood straight and tall, even though it had a big crack down the center. Mildred told me that she believed that this tree was another message from God that she could be strong and whole, even with her physical imperfections. She told me, "If the torn woman and that big tree are reflections of God, then God must have wounds too. So why should I think I have to be perfect to hold my head up high?"

The cancer experience leaves people with many physical wounds that affect their whole body, mind, and spirit. As their bodies suffer disfigurement and impairment, questions arise concerning their identity and worth as human beings. The identity crisis that many people endure challenges their hoping capacity. Struggling to make sense of who they are in the present with all the changes they have endured, they may despair of seeing their dreams realized in the future. Pastoral counselors have the opportunity to take part in the restoration of hope. Hearing their stories of pain and grief from the changes their bodies have suffered begins the process. Connecting their stories with other sacred stories, including our own stories of woundedness, may further restore their image of themselves as whole persons, regardless of their losses. The movement toward wholeness continues through pastoral interventions that invite people to imagine God as wounded. The image of a Divine Lover who suffers with them and thus understands all their struggles brings comfort and healing. The Wounded Healer, imaged in the form of a human being or of the earth, brings Divine Presence close to people with cancer, empowering them to move toward the reciprocal process of receiving and giving healing. Believing that they are in the image of the Divine, even in their imperfections, inspires them to walk into the future with hope and power.

Chapter Eight

What Treatment Should I Choose? The Ethical Dilemma

Walking through the maze,
with no compass,
I rush ahead, looking down one path,
and then another, only to find
another and another every way I turn.
Can I take more than one?

Choosing the wrong way does not
just mean success or regret,
but life or death.
So I look frantically all around
in every direction, shouting,
"Won't somebody please tell me where to go?"

Taking the right paths may demand
more than all that I have.
As time for choosing runs out,
I stand paralyzed in the maze, looking
in all directions, praying
for Divine Wisdom to lead me out.

Television actor Bill Bixby went through an intense struggle with prostate cancer. In addition to enduring surgery, chemotherapy, and experimental hormone treatment and their side effects, he agonized over personal choices concerning his vocation and his relationships. When reporters asked Bixby what his most difficult challenge had been throughout the ordeal, he replied, "Without question, it was trying to decide what to do about treating the cancer. It's a maddening, mysterious disease. Each case is unique, and you get a bewildering amount of conflicting information and opinions."[1]

Choosing among treatment options for any kind of cancer is challenging. When physicians disagree about the efficacy of various treatments, the task is especially daunting. In support groups, people with various cancer diagnoses often talk about feeling bewildered when they discussed their treatment options with surgeons and oncologists. Trying to comprehend all the information concerning the benefits and risks of different treatments shortly after hearing their cancer diagnosis was staggering. One man talked about his ambivalent feelings as he tried to listen to his physician present the options: "In a way I just wanted my doctor to tell me what to do. That would have made it so much easier. But at the same time I wanted to maintain some control, so I knew I had to work as hard as I could to gather information and make a responsible choice."

The controversy in recent years among medical professionals concerning treatment of prostate cancer increases the ethical dilemma for men diagnosed with this disease. These men and their families must weigh the risks and benefits of surgery, radiation, chemotherapy, and hormone therapy. Aggressive treatment may increase survival chances for some, but at the risk of loss of sexual function and loss of bladder control. Although watchful waiting, as opposed to any treatments, is controversial, a high percentage of U.S. physicians concede that it is a viable option for most men over seventy with early-stage prostate cancer. Whether or not watchful waiting is a prudent option for men under seventy is much more controversial. The United States and several other countries have begun major clinical trials to determine whether watchful waiting or surgery is the better option for men under seventy.[2] Meanwhile, men with prostate cancer and their families often feel that they are playing a guessing game with extremely high stakes. About a year after he went through surgery and radiation, one man in his early sixties learned that his prostate cancer had spread to his bones. His surgery had left him incontinent and impotent. He lamented, "If I had it to do over again, I wouldn't have surgery. I've given up so much, and all for nothing."

People diagnosed with breast cancer may also find the choices of treatment overwhelming. One woman told me that of all the devastating feelings she suffered when she was diagnosed with breast cancer, the most difficult was the anxiety over her decision about treatment. Receiving contradictory opinions from four physicians increased her anxiety. She felt that she had to consider not only which treatment offered the greatest chance of cure, but also which offered the highest quality of life. She wondered whether her psychological response to lumpectomy would be better than to mastectomy.[3] Even if she accepted the opinion of the physician who said that she had the same chances for cure with lumpectomy as with mastectomy, she also had to consider whether or not saving her breast was worth going through the six weeks of radiation therapy she would need along with the lumpectomy. To help her make her decision, she used the Internet to gather opinions from other women who had been through this experience.

The number of treatment possibilities for people with cancer continues to increase. Along with the conventional treatments of surgery, radiation, chemotherapy, and hormone therapy, experimental treatments are available for some types of cancer. In addition, there is a plethora of alternative and complementary therapies that many people consider. During the months and years following a cancer diagnosis, many people face repeated choices about treatment. Selecting the most appropriate options may determine survival chances and/or quality of life. Many lives have been saved or lost as a result of the quality of decisions people make concerning their cancer treatments. People with cancer realize that the stakes are high, and thus they may feel deeply conflicted as they face choices among treatment options.[4]

In choosing among treatments, people must balance chances for cure against undesired side effects. A year after undergoing extensive chemotherapy and marrow transplantation in treatment of lymphoma, one middle-aged man suffered a recurrence. He agonized over the option of another transplant that promised little chance of long-term survival and that would decrease his quality of life. He wondered if the painful side effects he would suffer with another aggressive treatment were worth the small chance of more time. And he knew that even though this treatment might eradicate the cancer, there was a possibility that he might die from the side effects of the treatment.

Many people consider experimental treatment when their cancer does not respond to standard interventions. When they have exhausted all conventional treatment, they may look frantically for physicians investigating new therapies. Their hope for a cure may be revived when they learn of exciting new research in biological therapies, such as immunotherapy and gene therapy. In the future, immunotherapy may provide a cure or at least change the nature of cancer from a progressive and lethal disease to one that can be controlled throughout a long life.[5] Gene therapy holds the potential of being more effective and less toxic than conventional therapies.[6] But these therapies are still in various stages of clinical trials. People choose to enter these trials with no guarantees that they will increase either the quantity or the quality of their lives. They may suffer the disappointment of being rejected for such trials because their physical condition or personal characteristics prove incompatible with the experimental design. People who are accepted into clinical trials usually place more hope on these experimental treatments than do physicians and scientists. Some investigational therapies are new enough that little data is available regarding benefits and side effects. Many people undergoing these treatments demonstrate the human capacity to hope against all odds. The hope that they derive from the experimental treatment may itself contribute to extending the quantity as well as the quality of their lives. They also express a sense of satisfaction from the knowledge that they are participating in a study that may contribute to scientific progress and thus help people in the future.

People with cancer seek alternative treatments for a variety of reasons: they have no other options of conventional or experimental therapies; they do not trust conventional or experimental treatments; alternative therapies appear to offer greater benefits with fewer side effects; they want more direct control over their lives than conventional medicine offers; they want these treatments along with conventional therapies in order to feel that they have done everything they can do. People who choose alternative cancer treatments are usually well-educated and reflect the social concerns of personal responsibility, caring for the environment, and prevention of disease.[7] Whether to choose alternative therapies may pose a difficult ethical dilemma because few of these therapies have been tested in scientific trials, and they may turn out to be costly, useless, or even dangerous.[8] It is often hard to discern whether the people promoting these therapies are exaggerating their claims and taking financial advantage of vulnerable people or whether they are motivated by altruistic concern.

Instead of an either-or choice between conventional and alternative therapy, many people choose both. Complementary therapies, including nutritional and psychosocial treatments along with conventional treatment, are increasingly becoming the focus of research studies. These studies seek to determine improvement in quality of life as well as prolonged survival rates. In the meantime, people with cancer often feel overwhelmed as they try to explore all the treatment possibilities and to examine their claims. Family and friends may add to the stress by their recommendations of therapies they have heard or read about.

People with cancer may feel that they are trapped in a maze with no guiding compass to direct them to the right paths. Pastoral counselors can play an important role in helping people to discover that compass within themselves. An important pastoral intervention is to help people clarify the theological, philosophical, cultural, and personal values that affect ethical decision making. Chaplains and pastoral counselors can serve as facilitators of open communication and mediators when the values of people with

cancer clash with the values of their families or of the medical staff.[9] Within
the context of these value systems, people wrestle with questions concerning cost of therapies versus benefits. Can life be prolonged? If so, for how
long? Will suffering be relieved or increased? Will the treatment improve
or diminish the quality of life? How will others related to the person taking the treatment be affected?

In helping people with cancer find guidance through the decision-
making process, pastoral counselors can call on the rich heritage of theological ethics in combination with medical ethics. The relational model
of covenant forms the foundation for the ethical vision set forth in the
Hebrew and Christian scriptures. This covenant is a sacred bond or relationship between human beings and a greater power. Such an ethical vision motivates and guides people to a consideration of the well-being of
others and to the stewardship of all life.[10] A theology of God's all-inclusive,
unconditional love for creation leads to ethics based on the worth and
dignity of all life. This ethical vision requires justice in all relationships
and endeavors. In making ethical decisions, we must then consider the
good of the community along with the good of the individual. Images of
God as inclusive Love and Justice inform the person with cancer and the
pastoral counselor as together they seek solutions to difficult ethical
dilemmas.

Medical ethics has traditionally followed certain principles for decision
making. A classic ethical principle in medical decision making is beneficence. Based on the Hippocratic principle, beneficence guides health care
professionals to benefit the patient according to their ability and judgment.
Some, seeing the paternalism inherent in this model, have placed autonomy
at the center of medical ethics. Autonomy, defined as respect for the individual's right to self-determination, has become popular as a guide to medical decision making, especially in the United States. Some ethicists, instead
of asking health care professionals to abandon their historical position of
beneficence, call for a balancing of this principle with the principle of autonomy. Thus the central values guiding decision making are the patient's
well-being and respect for the patient's self-determination.[11] Honesty is
another important ethical principle, requiring that health care professionals be truthful in communicating information about treatment options so
that people can make informed decisions. There is increasing emphasis on
the ethical principle of justice, defined as fair distribution of resources. The
issue of the just allocation of resources brings into focus the good of the
community as well as the individual. Eric Cassell believes that "autonomy
itself implies a social world" and that the emphasis on autonomy in the recent past has obscured the communal aspect of individuality, particularly in
academic ethics.[12] Judith Caron asserts that ethics and morality have always
"involved a tension between the individual and the community as a whole.

From primitive times, human beings have learned that basic survival needs can only be met when people band together in shared efforts."[13]

The advent of managed health care heightens the tension between the individual and the community by bringing an increasing number of parties into clinical decision making. Ethical issues that once concerned only health care professionals and patients have expanded to include groups who manage care, such as health maintenance organizations (HMOs) and preferred provider organizations (PPOs). Managed care is a response to many problems within the American health care system, including uncontrolled costs and unfair allocation of resources. But managed care can create other problems if providers of health care, health care institutions, and managed care organizations become more interested in their own financial gain than in the welfare of human beings. Managed care may threaten autonomy and beneficence if HMOs carry the greatest authority for medical decision making.

In addition to the social ethical concerns regarding the just allocation of limited resources, environmental concerns are also important to biomedical ethics based on a theology of the goodness of all creation.[14] Guided by this theological ethical vision, pastoral counselors advocate a medical decision-making process in which all involved, including managed care organizations, are motivated by the best interests of individuals and by a careful stewardship of resources, not by an incentive to undertreat in order to maximize profits. In addition to articulating principles that apply to individual cases, those involved in medical decision making need to address the influence of institutional structures on the allocation of health care resources. We must ensure that the health care system affords access for all and that it exercises responsible stewardship of the earth's resources.[15]

Verna, a single, middle-aged woman diagnosed with multiple myeloma, struggled with ethical dilemmas that grew out of her managed care organization's capitation on coverage of a treatment recommended by her physicians. She agonized over whether or not to choose an aggressive treatment that her insurance would not fully cover. Since an initial chemotherapy treatment did not achieve a remission, Verna's physicians recommended high-dose chemotherapy and radiation followed by a marrow transplantation. Verna understood her physicians' explanations that this treatment was her only chance of survival. When I saw her for counseling, she expressed her anxiety over the financial burdens of the treatment. Her insurance company would pay for in-patient treatment but not for out-patient prescriptions that could cost as much as $1500 a month. Recovering from the transplant might require her taking these prescriptions for several years.

One of Verna's strongest personal values was fulfillment of responsibilities. She had been single for almost twenty years and had reared a daughter by herself. Verna valued her independence and her ability to meet her financial obligations. A health care professional, Verna approached her decision about the transplant realistically, understanding its possibilities and limitations. She knew that it offered no guarantees of long-term survival, and she understood the cost in terms of suffering as well as finances. Her family, coworkers, and church friends could not understand Verna's dilemma; they believed without question that she should have the aggressive treatment because it was her only chance of survival. They pressured her to choose the transplant, telling her that money should not even be a consideration. Because her family and friends were important to her, Verna valued their opinions.

Verna's theological and philosophical beliefs also entered into her decision-making process. Her belief that "God gave me a disease I can't afford" conflicted with her belief that God expected her to take responsibility for her disease. But at the same time she believed in God's miraculous intervention in her life. She was trying to seek divine guidance in making her decision about treatment. In our session, I tried to help her to understand competing values and beliefs that were causing her conflict and then to discover God's leadership in this decision.

VERNA: I was hoping and praying that I could get by without the transplant. But now that I'm getting worse I understand that this is my only chance. I'm just totally bewildered. How can I choose this transplant when I can't afford it? You know my insurance won't pay for my medications when I leave the hospital, and I have to have them to survive the transplant. Everybody keeps calling me and telling me what to do, but I just don't know. They say I've got to have the transplant and not to worry about the cost, that they can help me raise the money. Do a fund-raiser, they say. But I don't even have the energy to think about that now, and I've never had an outgoing personality. (*crying*) It all seems so bewildering. I've got to think about the cost. I can't afford it, and I don't want to put that kind of burden on my family.

PASTORAL COUNSELOR: Verna, it sounds as though your family is very important to you. You value their opinions, and you value your financial independence. These two values may be causing some conflict in you.

VERNA: What do you mean?

P.C.: You want to consider your family's wishes for you to have the transplant, but you don't want to depend upon them to help you with out-patient medications.

VERNA: You're right. I've never believed in asking my mother or my brothers and sisters for help, not even after my divorce and I had a baby to take care of. I accepted my own responsibility, and I made it. My daughter's twenty-three now, but she has no way to pay for my medications. I just don't know what to do. God gave me a disease I can't afford. But I know God will help me through this.

P.C.: So you believe God gave you this disease and you can't afford the treatment, but at the same time you believe God will somehow help you?

VERNA: That may seem contradictory, but let me tell you the whole story. I had been feeling bad about eight months before I was diagnosed with cancer. I kept going to one doctor and another, and they misdiagnosed me. The pain in my back and legs was so bad that I had to miss work for many weeks. I used up all my vacation days and my disability. When I was finally diagnosed, I was out of money. My pain was getting worse, and I had to begin chemo treatments. So I had to miss work without pay. I had no money for rent or anything else. But God took care of me. My coworkers and friends collected money for me, and they also helped me get money from a charitable foundation. Miraculously, I made it financially. I believe God has led me this far and won't leave me now.

P.C.: Your story of God's financial help in the past gives you assurance of God's help in the future.

VERNA: I know God will take care of me.

P.C.: Does that experience give you any guidance about the decision you're struggling with now?

VERNA: I guess I'm supposed to go ahead with the transplant and trust God to provide the money. Maybe one thing I'm supposed to learn through all this is to put more trust in God.

By recalling a sacred story in her past, Verna was able to find guidance to make the difficult decision concerning treatment. As she explored her values concerning her family, her financial independence, and her faith in God, she discovered that putting her trust in God took precedence. Hope for her future story came through this trust. Later as she was going through the treatment, she told me, "Whether I live or die, I'm sure of God's love. I know God will always take care of me."

In addition to helping Verna clarify her values in order to reach a decision about treatment, pastoral intervention included advocating changes within the system that caused Verna's ethical dilemma. I joined nurses and social workers involved with Verna in addressing the problem of the managed care organization's paying for an aggressive in-patient treatment but failing to pay for out-patient medications that were necessary to the success of the treatment. With her permission, I also presented her case to a conference of health care professionals examining ethical issues and managed care.

Since the mid-1960s, the National Cancer Institute (NCI) has become increasingly concerned with the avoidable mortality problem. The NCI identified a wide variety of "social barriers" to cancer detection and treatment. Socioeconomic factors limit access to care for many people. Some people die unnecessarily from cancer because of their inability to pay for health care or to negotiate an increasingly complicated system of specialists and hospitals.[16] Questions concerning access to health care are an important part of ethical decision making. The ethical principle of justice guides us to seek access to life-giving health care for all, regardless of their income or their social status.

Nineteen-year-old Tracy went to a hospital emergency room because her bleeding would not stop after her boyfriend hit her several times. Having a history of abuse, Tracy minimized her boyfriend's abusive behavior. Tracy had been reared by a grandmother who was physically abusive to her. Her mother, an alcoholic, and her father, a drug abuser, were rarely there for her. Her father once attempted to rape her and fired a shot at her. Her grandfather and the boyfriend of her aunt also attempted to rape her. Tracy attempted suicide when she was twelve and then again when she was fourteen.

Emergency room physicians diagnosed Tracy with leukemia and recommended that she see an oncologist right away for thorough tests and treatment. Tracy had no job or insurance. She had two children, ages two years and seven months. She had two sisters, but she was not close to them. Tracy's stepfather, who had helped support her and her children, had recently lost his job. Her main support was from her boyfriend, who had a minimum-wage job. Because she had no way to pay for treatment and had no knowledge of financial resources that might be available to her, she did not go to the oncologist. About a month later when she went back to the emergency room with high fever and bleeding, she was admitted to the hospital for treatment.

While Tracy was in the hospital, social workers helped her to apply for Medicaid coverage of her treatment. After she became stabilized, Tracy was discharged from the hospital and referred for weekly out-patient chemotherapy treatments. Her compliance with this treatment regimen was sporadic. When nurses confronted her about the dangers of this behavior, she showed little concern about the seriousness of her condition. Some health care professionals saw ethical problems in offering Tracy a treatment that she compromised by her noncompliance. Pastoral intervention included helping the staff understand how Tracy's socioeconomic and cultural background contributed to her behavior. As the empathy of her caregivers increased, Tracy began to follow the treatment program. Tracy even begin to look forward to coming for treatments because she experienced more love and care from some of the nurses than she had ever experienced before. Another pastoral intervention, in partnership with social workers, was to provide extensive counseling to guide Tracy toward self-worth. Because of Tracy's history of abuse and neglect from parents, images of God as Mother or Father were not helpful. Tracy could more easily feel divine love and her own value through images of God as Nurse, caring for her and working for her best interest.

Many people with cancer confront the question of whether or not to continue pursuing a treatment that does not appear to be working. Some will undergo weeks of intensive treatment for a chance of prolonging life by six to twelve months even if there is no hope for cure. But others refuse such treatment because of quality-of-life concerns and other considerations.

After undergoing extensive chemotherapy and radiation treatments for six months, Clarence learned that his lung cancer had spread to his brain. Physicians told Clarence that they could give him another kind of chemotherapy for six weeks, but that it would offer no chance of long-term survival. At best, it could extend his life by six months to a year. Since his immune system was still compromised from his recent chemotherapy treatments, this treatment would make him more susceptible to life-threatening infections. In addition, he would probably suffer the side effects of nausea and severe mouth ulcers as he had with previous chemotherapy treatments. He would likely spend a good part of his remaining time in the hospital.

Clarence discussed with me his dilemma over whether or not to choose this treatment. His wife and grown children wanted him to do everything possible to continue to "fight" the disease. Clarence told me that he had always been a "fighter," but that he did not think this treatment was going to help him conquer the cancer. And he had learned that he had reached the limit of his insurance coverage. His wife wanted to sell their house to pay for the treatment, but he did not think that would be right.

CLARENCE: You know I'm a fighter, but I've got to be sure I'm doing the right thing by my wife. She wants me to fight this cancer, but it's not right to leave her broke when my odds of winning are next to nothing.

PASTORAL COUNSELOR: It sounds as though your fight now is to do the right thing.

CLARENCE: Yeah, and how can it be right to take this treatment that's just going to make me sicker and give me little or no extra time, when it will cost my wife so much. She says she doesn't want money to be an issue, but it is. And it seems so wasteful to have this treatment that probably won't help me when there're so many people out there who might be helped by treatment, but they can't afford it. I don't think God wants me to do this; it just doesn't feel like the responsible thing to do.

P.C.: You see God as wanting you to be responsible to your family and others. You want to do the right thing in using resources. Maybe you can help your family understand your feelings about being a good steward.

CLARENCE: I don't want them to feel guilty in any way. I want them to know that they did everything they could and I did everything I could.

Clarence made the decision not to have the treatment he considered futile and wasteful. Imaging his relationship to God as that of responsible steward helped him to explain his decision to his family so that they could bless it.

People with cancer face decisions concerning life support procedures if their conditions become terminal and irreversible. Some choose to express their wishes in advance directives (living wills), while some find considering such possibilities too painful. Those who choose very aggressive therapies, such as marrow transplantation, are often more reluctant to sign directives to limit life support procedures.

Marshall, a middle-aged married man, received a marrow transplant from an unrelated donor in treatment of his leukemia. Although he had several opportunities to sign a living will, Marshall chose not to do so because he wanted to make sure that everything was done to prolong his life. He stated, "I've chosen this aggressive treatment, because I choose life." Several weeks after his transplant, Marshall began to develop respiratory problems. A few days later he had to be moved to the intensive care unit and placed on a ventilator. Marshall seemed alert and anxious in spite of medications to relieve pain and relax him. After a month on the ventilator, Marshall's anxiety began to increase into panic attacks. At the end of the fifth week, physicians decided to see how Marshall would tolerate a few hours off the ventilator. After an hour, it was clear that he needed to be put back on the ventilator in order to survive. Even though he could barely get enough breath to speak, he begged his wife, his mother, his father, and his brother not to put him back on the ventilator. Marshall also told me that he believed that he was dying and that he did not want to be put back on the ventilator. He said that he believed God wanted him to die. He asked me, "Do you believe it is wrong for me to give up?"

Physicians told the family that they believed Marshall still had a chance of survival, and they recommended that he be put back on the ventilator.

His mother, father, and brother concurred in spite of Marshall's pleas because they believed that the medications he was taking made him incapable of making a rational life-and-death decision at this time. His brother believed that Marshall should be put back on the ventilator so that God could perform the miracle of healing for which he had been praying. His wife felt deeply ambivalent about the decision as to whether or not to put Marshall back on life support. She wanted to give Marshall every chance to live, but she could not bear to ignore his pleas. My pastoral role was to facilitate communication that would identify personal, cultural, and spiritual values to guide their decision making.

Important to Marshall's value system was being in control. He had worked for twenty years as an insurance claims adjuster. He had functioned successfully in this structured, methodical job. Being able to "fix things" was important to him. I raised the question as to whether Marshall's request not to be put back on the ventilator was influenced by his anxiety over his loss of control of all aspects of his life, even his breathing. Perhaps he felt that the only choice he had left was to refuse life-sustaining treatment. His family continued to believe that the medication was guiding his request, since he had expressed his "true wishes" when he resisted signing an advanced directive.

Important spiritual issues were also involved in this ethical dilemma. Marshall was a member of a conservative Christian denomination that emphasized submission to God's will. Belief in an afterlife was another vital part of his theology. He held the strong belief that when he died, he would go to heaven. Marshall's question to me, however, implied his struggle over whether or not he would be going against God's will if he refused further treatment. Implied in his question to me was also a cultural belief that "giving up" might constitute failure. From his culture he had internalized the message of the virtue of fighting to the bitter end. His family was also giving him the message to keep on fighting and never give up. His brother's charismatic faith contributed to this message. He believed that Marshall should not give up because God was going to perform a miracle of healing. Every night his brother spent several hours reading biblical accounts of healing miracles to Marshall. Although the other members of the family did not belong to a charismatic denomination, they too encouraged Marshall to believe that God was going to heal him.

Open communication among all involved in this decision resulted in a consensus to put Marshall back on the ventilator. Marshall slowly recovered his respiratory function, and within a year was fully recovered from his leukemia. As it turned out, Marshall's family was right that his mental status, altered by medication, was driving his request not to be placed back on the ventilator. Although Marshall appeared alert when he made this request, he later had no memory of the request. The simplistic approach would have been to consider only the ethical principle of autonomy and to honor

Marshall's request without deliberation. If that had been done, Marshall would have died when his life could have been saved. Ambiguous ethical issues require careful examination and open communication concerning complex psychosocial, cultural, and spiritual dimensions of the issues.

The challenge of determining the right care is one of the most difficult dilemmas that people with cancer and all those involved with them regularly face. They struggle to choose between conservative and aggressive interventions. When conventional therapies are not working, people wrestle with whether to choose experimental or alternative treatments or both. The decision becomes especially difficult when they have gone through various treatments and not achieved a remission.

Three months after her stem cell transplant, Peggy (see chapter 4) had a series of tests that showed her cancer to be still active. Peggy's conversation with her oncologist confirmed her worst fears. The cancer had not responded to the high-dose chemotherapy and transplant. The oncologist said that there was nothing more she could do for Peggy. Determined to live, Peggy began to explore other options. She went to see several other oncologists for their opinions. One offered another chemotherapy regimen, but he was cautious about promising any benefits from this treatment. Wanting to maintain some sense of control, Peggy explored alternative and experimental treatments. When she came for pastoral counseling, she was distraught as she tried to make the right decision concerning treatment.

PEGGY (*crying*): I feel so all alone. When I was having conventional treatment, I felt that my doctors helped me make decisions. Now I feel like I'm on my own as I'm trying to look at alternative and experimental treatments. It's so hard because I know this is a life-and-death decision. Also I have to consider quality of life for myself and for Tom [her husband]. Is it worth exhausting all our financial resources for just a small chance that the treatment might help? (*crying increases*) Should I just turn everything over to God and quit trying to take so much responsibility? Maybe I've been too controlling and not trusted God enough. I hear sermons on "let go and let God," but something keeps me from doing that. Does my taking responsibility for decisions about my treatment mean I'm not trusting God?

PASTORAL COUNSELOR: Maybe it can be both-and, instead of either-or. What if you saw yourself in partnership with God? You do your part, as you have been, learning as much as possible about treatment options, and then trust Divine Wisdom to guide your choices.

PEGGY: I know we've talked about that image of Divine Wisdom, and I like that. I hadn't thought about the concept of partnership with God, but that might be helpful.

P.C.: That's been a meaningful image for me. You may discover other images that have meaning for you.

PEGGY: Come to think of it, the idea of partnership feels better than thinking I've got to do it all or that I've got to turn it all over to God. Something happened just this week that feels like what you're talking about. My oncologist called and told me that I qualified for an experimental treatment. A month ago she had told me there was nothing more she could do for me. I refused to accept that and started searching for something myself. One of the things I found was a clinical trial that sounded like it might help me. I talked to my oncologist's nurse about it, and she said I might qualify for it and that she would send blood samples and my medical records to the director of the study. If I hadn't taken it upon myself to do research on clinical trials, I wouldn't have this option now. But it's still a hard choice because it offers only a slight chance of a cure, and the treatment will be strenuous. Also I'll have to spend a lot of money flying every week to the center that's doing this research study. Even if I get a little extra time, I might have side effects that would keep me from enjoying it. As I was going through all this agony of looking at this option and other options of alternative treatments, I had an experience that's hard to describe. I was in the shower, of all places. I felt this Presence surrounding me and then a deep sense of trust filled me. It was as though I knew everything would be all right, whatever decision I made. This feeling didn't last long, but it was so powerful—more than I can tell you. (*crying*) I wish I could stay there, but now I'm back on the floor, not knowing which way to turn.

P.C.: Peggy, your story is very moving. Maybe it can give you some direction. Your almost simultaneous experiences of doing all you can and then feeling a deep trust can guide you as you make decisions about your treatment now. When you feel that you've done all you can to learn about your options, then trust Divine Wisdom to be your partner in making the right choice.

At the beginning of our session the next week, Peggy told me that thinking about being in partnership with Divine Wisdom had helped her make the decision to enter the clinical trial and to pursue a complementary nutritional therapy. She had thoroughly read the information on the clinical trial and had also had a consultation with a nutritional specialist. Peggy then called the director of the research study and asked additional questions, including whether she could use the nutritionist's recommended therapy to support herself during the treatment. When she prayed about the decision, she felt "guided toward this experimental treatment and very peaceful." She told me that she felt she had "moved to a new level of trust." She did not feel obsessed about whether or not the treatment would work. She was not putting her trust in the treatment, as she had done with the stem cell transplant.

The choices people with cancer make spring from their deepest resources of body, mind, and spirit. Realizing the life-and-death importance of these decisions increases the anxiety they feel as they try to do the right thing. These decisions also have far-reaching effects on others in their relational network. People with cancer may feel so overwhelmed, confused, and anxious about their options that they despair. Pastoral counseling can help them to search their sacred stories to find some compass to guide them. Often by recalling a story in their past, they clarify an ultimate value or belief that helps them resolve the current dilemma with insight and courage. As they integrate their deepest spiritual beliefs into their decision making, they can envision a hopeful future story.

As people are exploring the wide variety of treatment options, pastoral counselors can invite them to envision God in a variety of forms and images. If they can see that Ultimate Reality takes many forms, they may be able to expand their thinking about the decisions before them. They may not then restrict themselves to a simple "either-or" choice, but may consider choosing "both-and" treatments. For example, they may choose alternative therapies to complement conventional therapies. Pastoral counselors can suggest sacred images that enable people to make difficult ethical decisions with confidence. The image of Divine Wisdom as their partner can give them power to explore all their options and to act decisively, while experiencing the peace that comes from knowing that at the same time they can trust a Higher Power to guide them. Seeing God as a Nurse who cares for all and works for the best interest of all inspires an ethical vision of universal access to health care. Images of God as all-inclusive Love and Justice lead to an even broader ethical vision of connection with all creation and stewardship of all life. Such an expansive ethical vision challenges pastoral counselors not only to guide people with cancer toward clarity and confidence in ethical decision making but also to advocate changes in the health care system and in the world community so that all life experiences wholeness.

Chapter Nine

How Much Time Do I Have?
The Many Faces
of Hope and Healing

More time, more time—
there has never been enough time.
How can there be enough time now
to savor all there is of life and love and beauty,
to smell each flower and taste each fruit?

Moving in time, carefully
and urgently because I do not know how much is left,
I hear voices all around me:
strange and distant voices,
as from another time and space.

Moving in a dimension beyond time
while still in time,
I cry out in labor,
as the Divine Midwife tenderly holds my hand
and sings a birthing song.

From the moment they first hear the word "cancer" applied to themselves, people enter a different dimension of time. The initial feelings of shock have a sense of timeless unreality. Time stands still as they try to grasp the dreadful reality. As they slowly face the sobering truth of their diagnosis, the future, which only a little while before had stretched out before them into open space, becomes suddenly nebulous and constricted. One of their most pressing questions is, "How much time do I have left?" The major existential issue faced by most people as they progress through the cancer experience is their own mortality. Whatever the stage of cancer and whatever prognosis they receive from physicians, they live with the reality that they have a life-threatening disease. People with cancer, no matter how long they have been in remission, live with the threat of a possible recurrence of their disease. The anxiety of living with this threat may challenge the hoping process. If treatment fails and the cancer spreads or recurs, a despair-hope crisis may occur. People often move through the crisis by changing the focus of their hope. Pastoral counselors have unique opportunities to guide people with cancer to reshape distressing future stories by helping them to see the many faces of hope and healing.

When first diagnosed with cancer, most people hope for a cure. Physicians and treatments often become the focus of their hope. They put all their energy into getting through the treatments and returning to life as they knew it before cancer. One young man said that when he was diagnosed with Hodgkin's disease, he had every reason to hope that radiation and chemotherapy would cure him, because everybody told him that this disease was curable. After several recurrences, he found it harder to hope for a cure. Some people, from the beginning, have trouble hoping for a cure. Such was true of a young woman when she learned she had breast cancer. Since she had watched her mother die of breast cancer, she had trouble believing that she could survive the cancer.

If it becomes obvious that the cancer is not responding to treatment, people often enter a time of examination and alteration of their goals and hopes for the future. When he learned that his lung cancer had not responded to any treatments, one man said that his hope "narrowed from a cure to extended time." Hope may center on more time to complete some important project or to experience some important event. Gradually people with cancer may change their focus from quantity to quality of life. Making every moment count may become their highest goal. Instead of longing to return to a past "normal" condition or looking forward to something in the distant future, life is lived more in the present tense. Instead of setting long-term goals, they may set more limited short-term goals. Letting go of an original hope of seeing their grandchildren, they may set a goal of just seeing their children graduate from high school. Some people live longer than they or their physicians ever thought possible by focusing on one short-term goal after another. One woman in her forties lived with metastatic breast cancer two years longer than physicians predicted. She kept hoping and living toward one more special occasion: a long-planned-for vacation with her family, one more Christmas and then another, her high school reunion.

A recurrence of cancer usually brings a modification, not a loss, of hope. A research study revealed that the average level of distress in people whose cancer had recurred was not significantly different from those who were newly diagnosed. In fact, some found that coping with the recurrence was easier than coping with the first diagnosis. Existential concerns, however, created a higher level of distress in people whose cancer had recurred than in those recently diagnosed. Those who had the most physical symptoms and disability reported the highest level of distress, but rarely expressed feelings of hopelessness. Highly distressed people reported having fewer support systems available than those with lesser degrees of distress.[1]

As cancer progresses, hope may focus on reconciliation of some relationship, alleviation of suffering, and the welfare of loved ones left behind. People may move on from these transitional hopes to a deeper, transcending hope for what may come after death.[2] Aspirations for immortality emerge in the form of desire to have individual life after death or to be part of the universe, as well as in the form of producing lasting influence through our work, our children, and our acts of service.[3]

Inherent in the hoping capacity is a sense of meaning, purpose, and identity. Disease and suffering may threaten a person's sense of purpose, or this central purpose may nurture hope in the midst of suffering. Suffering often comes from a fear of the future disintegration of personal identity.[4] Hope of continued identity in a life that transcends earthly life may bring meaning that helps relieve this suffering. One study demonstrated that in addition to the theme of finding meaning, four other central themes influence the hoping capacity through the cancer experience: reliance on inner resources, maintaining affirming relationships, living in the present, and anticipating survival. Inner resources include optimism, confidence, self-worth, self-determination, and humor. Drawing strength from family members and friends, as well as from health care professionals, is a helpful strategy in defining and sustaining hope. Living in the present involves appreciating each moment and having a sense of normalcy in everyday life. Aspects of anticipating survival important to hope include having treatment options, knowing a potential exists for a cure, and being in remission.[5]

Some people have difficulty finding any hope when they cannot anticipate survival. Glenda, a middle-aged woman diagnosed with pancreatic cancer, saw no reason to hope after her physician told her that she had "little or no chance of surviving this." For the past twenty years, Glenda, a research geologist, had devoted most of her time and energy to her vocation. Her identity and sense of purpose in life came mainly from her work. I tried to help Glenda reframe hope through discovery of some additional meaning.

PASTORAL COUNSELOR: Glenda, you've told me how much satisfaction you've gotten from your work. It's sounds as though you're a devoted scientist. Can you tell me more about the feelings you have when you're working?

GLENDA: The feeling of accomplishment my work gives me is wonderful. But there's something more that's hard to describe. I don't know if I've told you about my hobby—rock climbing. (*laughing*) I guess I just can't get enough of rocks! (*pointing to pictures on the bulletin board in her hospital room*) *There I am rock climbing with a good friend out in New Mexico.*

P.C. (*looking at the pictures*): You look radiant—like you're really in your element.

GLENDA: I have this connection with rocks—with the earth. Rock climbing, just like my work as a geologist, gives me this great feeling of being part of something bigger than myself. And now I have to give all that up. I can't do any of that anymore. There's nothing left.

P.C.: Glenda, you're grieving so many losses. It sounds as though you're able to find transcendence, some connection with a Higher Power through your work with nature.

GLENDA: I don't think I'd put it that way. I grew up in church, but I quit believing many years ago. My friends and family are praying for me now. I don't mind if they do. Sometimes I wish I could have that kind of simple faith, but I can't anymore.

P.C.: Maybe the ideas of God you grew up with are just not big enough for you anymore. Perhaps it would help you to think of God in the image of a stable and secure Rock that you feel connected with, or maybe some other image in nature would bring you hope and comfort.

GLENDA (*giving me an indulgent smile*): Perhaps, but I can't seem to have simple faith.

On several other occasions I tried to guide Glenda to tap into a sacred story or image that would give her some hope in the midst of her painful circumstances. I was hoping that she might expand the connection she felt with the earth to a connection with a Power greater than earthly life. Glenda never found a sacred image that gave her hope that there was anything beyond her suffering and losses. Reframing my hope for our pastoral relationship, I continued to visit Glenda and to invite her to tell me stories of her rock climbing. As she did so, the light in her eyes led me to believe she experienced a few moments of transcendence.

When they learn that their cancer cannot be cured, some people move the locus of hope from survival to discovery of new meaning in life. The news that they have a short time to survive may lead to a new level of self-actualization. Healing may come in the form of restoration of health, but it may also come in the form of recovery of a lost part of a person. It can mean surrender of illusions as the person becomes open to new values and experiences.[6] As his bone cancer progressed, one man said that he finally "threw off the shackles of superficial values, like money and success and prestige. Nourishing relationships is what matters, what's eternal." Contemplating mortality often changes life irrevocably.[7] A man struggling with liver cancer said that his illness had brought devastating pain, dependency, and fear, but that it had also been the means of a "powerful transformation." Knowing that his time on earth was limited had completely changed his daily experience. He had learned to live more fully in the present and to see the sacredness in simple things that he had previously overlooked.

Like all of Sacred Reality, healing comes in many forms, with many faces. Although people with cancer naturally hope for a physical cure, they often experience other forms of healing. As one woman with ovarian cancer learned more about the mind-body-spirit connection, she affirmed that whether or not she became well physically, "a healing is going on anyhow." Through her research and meditation, she discovered levels of herself that she had never known existed. She felt as though she were giving birth to a new self. John Carmody, a teacher of religion and a prolific author, describes similar experiences in his spiritual reflections on facing cancer and death. As he struggled with multiple myeloma, Carmody developed new aspects of his spiritual and creative self. He became more open to the feminine divine, finding comfort in the image of God as a gentle, welcoming Lover. Carmody felt a "new spirit" of creativity moving him "onto a new track" in his writing. The motivation of his creative work changed from external to internal, as he turned from writing what he felt obligated to write for others to writing what he was most drawn to. Never glossing over the stark reality of his suffering, Carmody made it clear that all this growth came not from passive acceptance but from hard work. As his disease progressed, he also began to experience time in a new way: "When I think of the absolute future, the end of the tunnel toward which my cancer is hurtling me, I sometimes realize that the future is now. The eschaton, the end-time, is this present, acceptable hour."[8]

A primary pastoral opportunity is to guide the person with cancer to see the many faces of hope and healing so that a new sense of self may emerge. Pastoral counselors can envision themselves as partners with the Divine Midwife in giving birth to this new self. Guiding people to shape their sacred stories with a view toward a future that holds possibilities of new birth is an important pastoral intervention.

After completing every recommended treatment for his lymphoma, including an experimental therapy, Bill (see chapter 3) learned that his disease was still progressing. Physicians told him that they had no other treatments to offer him. While grieving the loss of hope for a cure, Bill began to hope for some quality time at home with his wife and young son. He left the hospital with plans for nursing care in his home. A few weeks later his worsening condition brought him back to the hospital, where he spent the last month of his life, mentally alert until the last few days. During that month I visited with him almost daily.

On his good days, Bill talked with me at great length, first giving me the details of his present physical condition and then telling me stories from his past, including his vocational experience as a business executive and his experience growing up in a large Roman Catholic family. From there he would usually move to stories about his wife and son, focusing especially on his regrets that he had not spent more time with them and that he had not been more emotionally available to them. At first when he moved into these recitations of his failures, I would try to guide him to focus on the changes he was now making in these relationships. But after many days of his repeated litanies of relational failures, I realized how important this process was to his healing. In addition to storytelling, confession was a vital part of the ritual Bill and I performed together. Not only did Bill need to review his life story, but he needed to confess his past sins in order to be able to move on to a hopeful future story. To experience spiritual healing, Bill needed the ritual of forgiveness, as well as confession.[9] My pastoral intervention at this point was to follow his confession with a simple ritual of forgiveness, including scriptural assurances of forgiveness (1 John 1:9; Mark 2:5) and a prayer of thanksgiving for God's complete forgiveness.

After going through these rituals of confession and forgiveness on several occasions, Bill gradually let go of reciting his past failures. He became more open to my guiding him to include the present and future in his storytelling. Filling his room with pictures his son had colored, he would smile as he told me about each one. Short-term future stories of fun with his wife and son and of playing his guitar gave him purpose during these days. With the help of occupational therapists, Bill found pleasure in planning simple craft activities and movies he could enjoy with his wife and son. Playing the guitar was one of the things he had loved to do but had not taken time to do when he was a business executive. Even though his need for pain medications increased, he was amazed that there were times when he could not only play songs he had known before but could compose his own songs. Bill seemed to be tapping into a deep well of creativity that he had never known was within him. Even as his physical condition continued to deteriorate, another transformation I saw taking place was the growth of his philosophical imagination. During the last few years when he had been unable to work because of his illness, he had read extensively in philosophy and theology. Now he seemed to relish engaging me in conversation on philosophical issues, such as life on other planets or the immortality of the soul. One day as he was struggling with grief and fear, I invited Bill to use his imagination to envision the afterlife for himself.

PASTORAL COUNSELOR: Bill, I see you growing in so many ways. You're becoming a more whole person. You've integrated your intuition with your rational mind. Your creative imagination has come alive and helped you write songs. Also you seem to be growing in your capacity to imagine beyond the here and now. I wonder if you might want to imagine what your future will be like when you leave this world.

BILL: I believe in life after death, at least intellectually, but I have trouble imagining it. I guess I have some doubts and some fear when I try to think about eternity. But I'm more afraid of dying than of death itself.

P.C.: The dying process scares you?

BILL: It's hard for me to see past more and more pain. I see myself slowly disintegrating, losing control and losing everything. It feels like giving up everything, and I've never believed in giving up. (*voice breaking*) That's why I've fought this disease in every way I've known how. I went through every treatment I could, tried diet and vitamins, and you know how I prayed and tried so hard for a faith healing. But I guess I have to give all that up. There's nothing more I can do. All I can see ahead is more suffering.

P.C.: You're really hurting as you grieve all your losses. But what if you thought of yourself as letting go, instead of giving up? Instead of feeling that you're giving up on healing, what if you imagined letting go into a different kind of healing. Try to imagine with me for a little while that you're letting go into another world. You remember our talking one time about Coleridge and the supernatural themes of his poetry. He had this theory that the poetic imagination depends on a "willing suspension of disbelief." That is, in order to enter the world of the poem, we have to give up our disbelief in that imaginative world. This "suspension of disbelief" is the essence of poetic faith, according to Coleridge. Perhaps spiritual faith is like that. We have to suspend our disbelief in a world beyond this one and try with our imaginations to enter that other world. Will you try to do that?

BILL: Well, I guess I can imagine what I hope it will be like. (*long pause*) You know some people picture heaven as a place of perfect rest and contentment. The only activity they describe is singing praises to God and strumming harps. I like the part about the music, but perfect rest would not be heaven to me. (*laughing*) I can't imagine being happy just sitting around. You know, even since I haven't been able to work, I've been trying to do something. In some ways my mind has become more active as my body has slowed down. I love to read and learn new things. My vision of afterlife would be a place of continual learning and growing. (*becoming more animated*) Growing in every way—not just intellectually. I imagine it as a place where my spirit will expand and my talents will grow. Who knows what kind of music I may be able to write? Now this may sound strange, but I imagine being able to influence in some way what happens on earth, especially with people I love. I may not be able to communicate with them directly, but somehow I will maintain a connection. Maybe I could be like a guardian angel. I'd like to have some kind of assignment on earth or on some other planet. (*pausing, short of breath*) I imagine myself being able to travel freely around the earth and all around the universe, to be in some physical form but not limited by that form. I will be able to eat, and food will actually taste good! That'll be a welcome relief after all I've been through, but I won't have to eat to survive. It will be a place of exquisite beauty, filled with vivid colors. I will be able to enjoy all the sensual pleasures I've known on earth and many more. And, of course, nothing about me will ever deteriorate, only grow and expand. But I will never finish learning and growing. That would be too boring. You see, I do have quite an imagination! (*laughing*)

P.C.: You certainly do! That's a fascinating story of your future in another world. Your imagination is growing more lively! In fact, in many ways you seem to be growing toward greater wholeness.

BILL: That sounds hopeful. I think I'll try to stay with that "willing suspension of disbelief"!

Until his death several weeks later, Bill struggled to hold onto this hopeful future story in the midst of the distressing present reality of labored breathing and increasing pain. There was no linear movement toward complete acceptance, but a circular interplay of grief and fear and hope. He expressed gratitude for my continual reminders of his sacred story of a death-transcending future filled with growth and beauty.

While journeying with people through their sacred stories, pastoral counselors have opportunities also to encourage the exploration of divine images that open new doors of hope and healing. In my work with Peggy (see chapters 4 and 8) over many months as she went through inpatient and out-patient treatments, I gained deeper understanding and appreciation of the sacred power of the imagination. Peggy honestly and vividly articulated her experience with cancer, always receptive to my invitations to explore new concepts and images. Keeping a journal and meditation aided her internalization of images that she found comforting and empowering.

In one of our sessions before she had made her decision concerning experimental treatment, she struggled to express a feeling of unreality she had been having as she lived with uncertainty about how much time she had left. In some ways she felt that she was already outside this world, looking in.

PEGGY: It's such a strange feeling—really hard to describe. I may be in a group of people, like with friends when I was home for Christmas, and all of a sudden, I'm outside the group. I'm thinking this may be my last Christmas and this may be the last time I see some of these friends. I can still hear them talking and I still talk to them, but they don't really understand where I am and I'm not where they are anymore. Does that make any sense?

PASTORAL COUNSELOR: Let me try to understand. You feel that you're not really with them anymore—like you're in another place or another dimension? That must feel pretty lonely.

PEGGY (*with tears in her eyes*): It feels very lonely because I know there's no way they can understand what I'm going through. And I don't really want them to. It's too painful. Sometimes I feel this way with Tom (her husband) too. He tries to understand my feelings, but there's no way he can. And I don't want him to feel any more pain than he's already going through, fearing that he might lose me. It's like I'm still here, but not all here—another dimension is a good way to describe it. It feels strange.

P.C.: Your experience with cancer has moved you into a new dimension of life. Whatever happens from this point on, you'll never be the same.

PEGGY: And I'm glad. I don't want to go back to the person I was before. When I'm with my friends, so much of what they talk about seems so unimportant. I can't go back there, and I don't want to. But I'm not sure what's ahead. When I feel myself slipping away, I start thinking about eternity, and then I'm overwhelmed with fear and sometimes doubt. (*crying*) It helps me to think of the only time I've felt safe since my diagnosis—when I was on the marrow transplant unit. That felt like a womb. I was surrounded by people taking care of me. They took care of my every need and gave me so much hope.

P.C.: Maybe it would help you to imagine God like the marrow transplant unit where you felt safe, surrounded by love and care. The Bible describes the womb-love of God (Ex. 33:19; Isa. 46:3–4). Picturing God as a Womb, keeping you safe, may help you during this time.

In our next session, Peggy talked about how the image of God as a safe, secure Womb had helped her through her quandary over the experimental treatment. When she felt fearful about taking the treatment and about what she would do if she did not respond to this treatment, she imagined herself in the Womb of God. The more she felt she was able to trust God, the more she discovered about herself. She talked about discovering a much deeper, more spiritual self. Before her cancer experience, she had been the pragmatic one in the marriage. She had taken care of the finances and other details of her family's life. In her work as an accountant, she had been organized and efficient. She had always thought that her strengths lay more in her reasoning capacity than in her imagination. Although she had been a member of a church, she had never thought much about her faith. She never would have believed that she could have the conversations we had had in our counseling sessions. We talked about the changes she had made.

PEGGY: It's like I'm a different person. Before cancer, I never could have imagined some of the things we've talked about.

P.C.: You feel like a new person. In the time I've known you, I've seen many changes. You've expanded your imagination and your thinking about God and spiritual experience. You've learned to articulate your experience and feelings so vividly. I've learned so much from you.

PEGGY: I'm glad. That makes me feel good. You've helped me learn to trust more. I do trust God, no matter what happens. But I still hope for healing.

P.C.: Peggy, you're going to be healed one way or another.

PEGGY (*crying*): Yes, I know that.

P.C.: You're already experiencing healing and new life. As you've been telling me, you're becoming a new person. This picture of midwives might be helpful as you reflect on the new birth taking place within you. (*showing her a card with a picture, "The Midwives," by Doris Klein*) The artist writes these comments on the meaning of the picture: (*turning the card over and reading to Peggy*) "At times of passage we realize that God does not leave us alone, but sends midwives to accompany us and assist us on our journey. This painting reflects on the circle of women with whom God enfolds us as we experience the births and deaths of body, heart and spirit."[10] You might think not only of human midwives but also of God as the Divine Midwife helping you to give birth to new parts of yourself. There's a passage in Psalms that images God as Divine Midwife. "Yet it was you who took me from the womb; you kept me safe on my mother's breast" (Psalm 22:9).

PEGGY (*laughing*): You mean I can't just stay in the Womb?

P.C.: It seems to me that you're already moving out into something larger. (*giving her the picture*) I want you to have this picture.

PEGGY (*looking intently at the picture*): Thank you! This is beautiful and quite provocative. (*crying*) Thank you for giving me new ways of looking at what's happening with me and of imagining God with me.

Peggy continued to look at the picture and to talk about some of the feelings it evoked. In some ways she did want to remain in the safe Womb, because the transitions she was going through felt scary and lonely. But she also felt satisfaction over the changes she had made in her life and hope as she contemplated the new person she was becoming. At the conclusion of this session, Peggy asked me to pray for her.

P.C.: Spirit of healing, hope, and new life, you come to us in many forms and with many faces. You are the power within Peggy, giving her courage to trust you and giving her hope in new possibilities for herself. You are the one bringing healing to her, according to her deepest needs. You come to her through friends and family who care for her, through all those who serve as midwives in assisting her on her journey. You are the Divine Midwife helping her to give birth to new discoveries and new life within herself. Continue to labor with her as she becomes all you created her to be. Amen.

The next week Peggy began our counseling session by telling me that she carried the picture of "The Midwives" with her everywhere. She showed me where she kept it in her purse. Although this image brought her comfort and hope, she expressed dismay that these feelings did not last long. Most of the time she felt that she had a shroud around her and that there was nothing she could do to shake it off. The image of the shroud, which she knew to be death, dominated her thinking. She graphically described how the shroud colored everything she did, blocking her view of the future and keeping her from fully experiencing the present. Peggy pleaded for help in getting this shroud off. I suggested that she had taken the first step by talking about this ominous image. By naming it, she was exercising some power over it. I also recommended that she spend time in the next few days recording her feelings about this image in a journal, and then spend several days describing her picture of hope. She might even try drawing the two images.

Peggy brought her journal to our counseling session the next week. She first showed me two sketches she had drawn. Her picture of hope was of a young woman with long hair and a half smile. Hope's other facial features were indistinct. She wore a long, flowing gown. The other picture was her image of death in the form of a "bird-man," wearing a shroud. The most prominent features on the head of the bird-man were a beady eye and a long beak. The bird-man had a wide wing expanse and wore a large robe over his wings.

I asked Peggy if she would like to read her journal entries describing these two images. Her written descriptions were much more vivid and revealing than her drawings.

Hope looks young, maybe younger than I, but she is ageless. She's been around a long time. She stands very still, but she's not stiff. She's all in white, wearing a beautiful gown made of flowing material with a high bodice. She looks calm, serene, with an inner glow of knowing and happiness. She's not pushy like the bird-man. She doesn't talk like we do. You almost have to guess what she's thinking, but you always know that she is strong, that she is good and there's nothing that can happen that would make her go to pieces. Will I follow her to heaven? Why can't she answer me?

The journal entry describing hope then shifts to a list of desires. Here Peggy seems to be expressing her "hopes" for Hope.

Hope would be more verbal and more assertive with the darkness. Hope would let me see progress right away with the experimental treatment. Hope would calm my mind and heart without my having to work so hard to keep myself on an even keel. Sometimes I feel that I have to guess what

Hope is saying to me. Hope would talk to me in my language instead of almost telepathically. Hope would keep me company when I feel lonely and afraid and sad and washed away. Hope would take the pain away and would cure my cancer. Hope would reassure me all the time that the things I am doing to help myself would work this time and would not just join the list of things that I've tried and have failed.

Peggy then read to me her description of the "bird-man" image she had drawn.

He is half bird, half man. He looks more like a bird, but has human qualities. He can talk and move around. His robe is very expansive; it could cover me like a shroud in a moment, and I don't ever forget that. Sometimes he sits on my shoulder, and sometimes I can feel him in my chest near my heart. He always has an opinion, and it's always negative—makes me doubt life, myself, and everything to do with the illness. He's permanently perched on my shoulder, watching, always watching. I've been afraid to hope because it's always tempered by the actions of this whatever it is. I'm not in control; he is. I didn't ask for him to be here. He just kind of showed up, took up residence, and won't leave. His presence was always there but his image has crystallized over these many months. We're going to have to learn to coexist. He is death and can wrap me up in a shroud where it will be dark. I'll be alone, and no one will be able to find me. Will I be in hell, or am I already there? The bird-man's eyes are never covered. Sometimes it looks like he's sleeping, but he can sleep and observe at the same time. He always has a say in the way I'm feeling any time he wants to. If I'm in a mall, watching TV, even now. He says, "I'm here to stay. Don't ever forget I have the power to make you doubt, to make you fearful, to make you sad. I am your constant companion. If I choose to be quiet, you're lucky that time. I can press the accelerator and make life so painful for you that it feels like you're hanging onto a baby tree in a tornado for dear life—never knowing if the trunk will snap or be strong enough to hold on through the storm."[11]

After I expressed gratitude for the power of her imagination and verbal abilities that gave me deeper understanding of her experience, Peggy and I talked further about the longings and fears she had described through the images of the bird-man and Hope. The bird-man, with his constant presence and chattering, threatened to overwhelm Hope. Although Hope was strong and serene, she did not speak loudly and directly enough to keep the bird-man at bay. The bird-man exercised more power and control in her life than the elusive Hope. Peggy wanted to hear Hope's voice more clearly, but the bird-man kept drowning it out. Peggy asked for my help in her struggle to escape from the bird-man's power so that she could follow Hope. I suggested that Peggy might find Hope more in her intuitive than in her rational mind and that perhaps a guided meditation would help.

In the meditation I led Peggy to focus on her breathing and then to go in her mind to a place she had previously chosen for a meditation, the sacred place in her own backyard. In this place was a wooden deck where she sat surrounded by trees and brightly colored flowers. I suggested that she visualize Hope sitting beside her, smiling and speaking tenderly to her. Peggy could then express her deepest feelings to Hope, even though she knew Hope understood her completely even before she said a word. When the bird-man tried to interrupt their conversation, Peggy could tell him to fly off and then shake him off her shoulder. I suggested that she watch the bird-man slowly fly farther and farther away from her. Now she could listen to Hope and just enjoy being in her presence. I suggested that she imagine herself becoming more closely connected with Hope so that she could understand Hope's messages, no matter what language they came in, even if they came through silence. I suggested that she feel all her fears slowly fly out of her body, mind, and spirit as she felt perfect love and peace in the presence of Hope.

After the meditation, Peggy said that the image of the bird-man flying off her shoulder helped her feel that she had some control over him. Although she had wanted Hope to tell her more about the future, to help her see the big picture of her life, Peggy felt strong and peaceful with Hope sitting beside her. Peggy did not feel anxious about having Hope answer all her questions. Peggy told me that one of the most powerful moments in the meditation was a memory that came to her as she was sitting beside Hope. She remembered a brief vision she had had several months earlier when she was sitting on the deck in her backyard. It was a cloudy day, and she was feeling depressed. As she was looking up at the clouds, she had a vision of a door beyond the clouds. The door looked inviting, and she started to get up and move toward it. But she stopped, knowing that it was not yet time for her to go through the door. Peggy believed that during the meditation Hope brought back to her memory this vision of the door. She knew that the door was the entrance into a new dimension of life and that she would know when it was time to enter. One day she would follow Hope through the door.

A future story that brings courage to move into new dimensions does not have to be complete in its content. It may be only an outline, an image, a glimpse, a momentary vision. The vision of the door gave Peggy assurance of a future story beyond the door, even though she could not see the whole story. Pastoral guides have the holy calling of walking beside people with cancer as their stories unfold, encouraging them to move toward the many sacred possibilities of healing and new life. When they despair of the possibility of one kind of healing, we can invite them to open their eyes to see the other faces of healing. Reconciled relationships and recovery of lost parts of themselves may lead to new levels of being.

In partnership with the Divine Midwife, pastoral counselors may participate in the birthing of people with cancer into new dimensions of self and time. Helping them explore and transform their sacred images and stories, we offer hope through the long, arduous, painful process of labor. Through evoking the imagination, that connection between human and divine creativity, these stories and images hold power to illuminate present experience while moving that experience into timeless reality. Pastoral counselors have unique opportunities to guide people to move beyond what they can see by imagining future stories filled with hope in many forms, including the transformation of loss into growth and the transformation of death into new life. Through our empathic, creative contributions to these individual sacred stories, we participate in the larger story of the transformation of all creation.

> We know that the whole creation has been groaning in labor pains until now; and not only the creation, but we ourselves, who have the first fruits of the Spirit, groan inwardly while we wait for adoption, the redemption of our bodies. For in hope we were saved. Now hope that is seen is not hope. For who hopes for what is seen? (Rom. 8:22–24)

Appendix A:
A Ritual of Mourning Loss and Claiming Power

This ritual is most appropriate for a women's breast cancer support community that has been meeting long enough to build trust among members. Women whose diagnosis of breast cancer was at least six months earlier tend to have more insight into their losses and may thus be able to participate more fully in this ritual than those who have been recently diagnosed.

LEADER: We join to mourn losses suffered through breast cancer. We come to share one another's pain and to find meaning and hope through our shared feelings and experiences.

PARTICIPANTS: We connect as women who understand the meaning and power of our breasts. Our breasts make us feel feminine. Our breasts nurture new life. Our breasts bring pleasure to us and to our lovers. But our breasts can also bring us pain and danger. We have felt the pleasure of our breasts. We celebrate the life-giving power of our breasts. But we have also felt the life-threatening danger in our breasts.

LEADER: Though breasts can bring blessings, we know that they can also bring pain and illness.

PARTICIPANTS: We have felt the blessings of our breasts, but now we feel the pain of loss and the fear of the unknown.

LEADER: Breast cancer has brought fear and grief.

PARTICIPANTS: We fear not only for ourselves but for our families. An uncertain future lies before us all. We mourn our physical losses. We mourn the loss of our feelings of safety and security.

LEADER: As you feel the pain, contemplate the meaning of your loss. Each of you comes with individual feelings about your loss and its meaning. What does your loss mean to you? What does your breast mean to you? Choose an object or picture from this tray that symbolizes your loss.

Pass around a tray with these items on it: picture of a well-dressed woman; carton of milk; sexy bra; picture of a healthy, happy family; picture of a healthy woman in jogging suit. Invite each woman to talk about the object chosen and how it symbolizes her loss, or to talk about her loss in some other way meaningful to her.

PARTICIPANTS: Our breasts are important to us. They are important to our femininity, our sexuality, our nurturing capacity. We mourn our losses from breast cancer. We mourn the loss of our feelings of invulnerability.

LEADER: (*Pass an empty tray around, asking the women to put the object symbolizing their loss back on the tray.*) As you let go, feel the pain of loss. Mourn the loss of your breast and the other losses you have suffered from breast cancer.

PARTICIPANTS: We let go, feeling our pain and mourning our losses.

LEADER: As you continue to feel the significance of your losses and to grieve these losses, begin to think about your strengths beyond your losses. Choose an object from this tray that symbolizes your talents, strengths, creative interests, and/or goals for the future.

Pass around a tray with these items on it: craft materials, books, a briefcase, a cookbook, a journal and pen, sheet music, canvas and paints, a stethoscope, a computer disk. Invite each woman to talk about the object chosen and how it symbolizes her talents, creativity, interests, and/or goals for the future. Provide women the opportunity to talk about their strengths and goals in some other meaningful way if they do not connect with the symbols.

LEADER: (*Ask the women to hold in their hands the object symbolizing their talents, creativity, goals, and so on.*) As you continue to feel the pain and mourn your losses, hold fast your gifts, your talents, your goals and dreams for the future. You have suffered losses through breast cancer, but you have not lost your power as women. Claim your power, your full gifts as creators of beauty, as nurturers of life.

PARTICIPANTS: We are much more than our breasts. Our femininity and our sexuality do not depend upon our breasts. Our nurturing is not limited to our breasts. We have meaning, feminine strength, nurturing capacity, and creative powers far beyond our breasts. Our feelings of safety and security were only illusions. We can live life fully in the face of the unknown, realizing that the future is always uncertain. Even as we feel our pain and mourn our losses, we hold fast our talents and creativity. We embrace the gifts of each moment. We claim our power to create new beauty, to discover new meaning in life, to nurture ourselves and others toward fuller health and wholeness.

ALL: Source of all Comfort and Power, we seek your comfort as we mourn our losses, and your power as we gain new strengths. Open our eyes to discover new meaning and creativity within ourselves and others. Empower us to let go of the old and embrace the new as we grow toward all you created us to be. Amen.

Appendix B:
Guide to Pastoral Conversation Concerning Cancer and Spiritual Experience

1. Begin by asking people to talk about the feelings they had when they first learned that they had cancer. Guide them to compare these feelings at the time of diagnosis with their current feelings.

2. Invite people to talk about issues of meaning and purpose in relationship to their cancer experience. For example, do they place any special meaning on the cancer, or have they discovered any meaning and purpose through this experience?

3. Encourage people to talk about whether or not they feel God or a Higher Power is involved with them.

4. Guide people to talk about the connection between their spiritual beliefs and their feelings about themselves.

5. Move into discussion of spiritual questions or struggles raised by the cancer experience.

6. Invite people to talk about any changes in their religious or spiritual beliefs that have come with their experience of cancer.

7. Ask people to compare and contrast their experience of God since their cancer diagnosis with their experience before diagnosis. Suggest words to denote ways of experiencing God, such as close, distant, internal, external, caring, uncaring, aloof, blaming, forgiving, gentle, judging, loving, nurturing, punishing, peaceful, disturbing, predictable, mysterious, powerful, weak, protective, tender.

8. Move on to dialogue about images of God, drawing out comparisons of the ways people pictured and named God

before their cancer diagnosis with their pictures and names for God since diagnosis. Suggest images of God, such as Judge, Light, Guide, Father, Mother, Healer, Master, Friend, Rock, Creator, Destroyer, Lord, Chaos, Comforter, Ruler, Brother, Sister, Redeemer, Wisdom, Higher Power, Spirit, Nurturer, Sovereign, Sustainer, Love, Eagle, Fortress, Refuge, Great Physician, King, Holy One, Grandfather, Grandmother, Great Mystery.

9. Give people opportunity to tell stories of spiritual experiences that they have had since their cancer diagnosis.

10. Move to relational issues raised by the cancer experience. Talk with people about ways cancer has affected their relationships with family and friends and about spiritual images or experiences that have helped them with changes in relationships.

11. Invite people to talk about ways their experience with cancer has affected their physical and sexual identity and about images of God or spiritual experiences that have helped them to deal with changes in body image.

12. Guide people to talk about what they think their lives will be like in five years. Encourage them to include their fears and hopes for the future.

Notes

Introduction

1. Anne Lamott, *Bird by Bird: Some Instructions on Writing and Life* (New York: Doubleday, 1994), 185–94.

2. *A Cancer Sourcebook for Nurses*, ed. Claudette Varricchio, 7th ed. (Atlanta: American Cancer Society, 1997), 13.

3. *Cancer Facts and Figures—1996* (Atlanta: American Cancer Society, 1996), 1.

4. Henri J. M. Nouwen, *The Wounded Healer: Ministry in Contemporary Society* (New York: Doubleday, 1972), 95.

5. Andrew D. Lester, *Hope in Pastoral Care and Counseling* (Louisville, Ky.: Westminster John Knox Press, 1995), 3.

6. Jürgen Moltmann, *Theology of Hope*, trans. James W. Leitch (New York: Harper & Row, 1965), 25.

7. Elizabeth A. Johnson, *She Who Is: The Mystery of God in Feminist Theological Discourse* (New York: Crossroad, 1992), 3–4.

8. Janice Post-White, Carolyn Ceronsky, Mary Jo Kreitzer, Kay Nickelson, Debra Drew, Karen Watrud Mackey, Louann Koopmeiners, and Sarah Gutknecht, "Hope, Spirituality, Sense of Coherence, and Quality of Life in Patients with Cancer," *Oncology Nursing Forum* 23, no. 10 (1996): 1575.

9. William A. Fintel and Gerald R. McDermott, *A Medical and Spiritual Guide to Living with Cancer: A Complete Handbook for Patients and Their Families* (Dallas: Word Publishing, 1993), 183.

10. Jimmie C. Holland, "Cancer's Psychological Challenges," *Scientific American* 275, no. 3 (September 1996): 158.

Chapter 1.
Cancer: A Life-Shattering Diagnosis

1. James B. Ashbrook, "Living with Cancer as Fantasy and Fact: First Encounter," *Pastoral Psychology* 37, no. 2 (winter 1988): 76. Ashbrook worked for thirty-five years in pastoral care and counseling with cancer patients and then was diagnosed with lymphoma himself. Even though he was thoroughly acquainted with cancer and hospitals, he says he felt so stunned when he heard his diagnosis that he didn't have presence of mind to focus on what he needed or wanted to know when the doctor asked if he had any questions.

2. Avery D. Weisman, *The Coping Capacity: On the Nature of Being Mortal* (New York: Human Sciences Press, 1984), 15.

3. In the words of pastoral counselor Michael E. Cavanagh, few diseases "can cause so much physical pain, intellectual deterioration, emotional

devastation, social upheaval, and spiritual desolation as cancer." See "Ministering to Cancer Patients," *Journal of Religion and Health* 33, no. 3 (fall 1994): 238.

4. Judi Johnson and Linda Klein, *I Can Cope* (Minneapolis: DCI Publishing, 1988), 15–16.

5. Avery D. Weisman and J. William Worden, "The Emotional Impact of Recurrent Cancer," *Journal of Psychosocial Oncology* 3, no. 4 (winter 1985–86): 5–6.

6. A brief, clear discussion of the benefits and dangers of denial is found in Susan Nessim and Judith Ellis, *Cancervive: The Challenge of Life after Cancer* (Boston: Houghton Mifflin Co., 1991), 47–51.

7. Fawzy I. Fawzy and Nancy W. Fawzy, *A Structured Psychoeducational Intervention for Cancer Patients* (Cambridge, Mass.: Elsevier Science Publishing Co., 1994), 1.

8. In the case material I present, names of persons and some details included have been altered to protect confidentiality.

9. Wendy Schlessel Harpham, *Diagnosis Cancer: Your Guide through the First Few Months* (New York: W. W. Norton & Co., 1992), xi–xii.

10. Barrie R. Cassileth, Edward J. Lusk, Thomas B. Strouse, David S. Miller, Lorraine L. Brown, Patricia A. Cross, and Alan N. Tenaglia, "Psychosocial Status in Chronic Illness," *New England Journal of Medicine* 311, no. 8 (Aug. 23, 1984): 509.

11. Holland, "Cancer's Psychological Challenges," 158.

12. See Richard L. Schaper's "Pastoral Accompaniment of the Cancer Patient," *Journal of Religion and Health* 23, no. 2 (summer 1984): 139.

13. See Fawzy and Fawzy, *Structured Psychoeducational Intervention*, 2.

14. Cynthia McGinnis Richards and Edward L. Palmer, "Cancer and Humiliation: The 'Catch 22' of Disease," *Journal of Religion and Health* 30, no. 4 (winter 1991): 334–35. McGinnis Richards cites a study in which 73.6 percent of sixty-three adolescent cancer patients rated the effect of cancer treatment on physical appearance as extremely important.

15. See the discussion of cancer's devastating blow to feelings of control by psychologist Robert Chernin Cantor, in *And a Time to Live: Toward Emotional Well-Being during the Crisis of Cancer* (New York: Harper & Row, 1978), 10–14.

16. Richards and Palmer, "Cancer and Humiliation," 333.

17. Johnson and Klein, *I Can Cope*, 94–96.

18. See the discussion of emotional issues by physician and cancer survivor Wendy Schlessel Harpham in *After Cancer: A Guide to Your New Life* (New York: W. W. Norton & Co., 1994), 212–91.

19. Kathy LaTour, *The Breast Cancer Companion* (New York: William Morrow & Co., 1993), 331.

20. Quoted in Bill Moyers, *Healing and the Mind* (New York: Doubleday, 1993), 334. See also Morton Kelsey, *Transcend: A Guide to the Spiritual Quest* (New York: Crossroad, 1981), 193.

21. Cantor, *And a Time to Live*, 223.

22. Colin Ryder Richardson, *Mind over Cancer* (New York: W. Foulsham & Co., 1988), 50.

23. See Lois A. Lorenz and Frank L. Sullivan, "The Initiation Ritual as a

Model for Oncology Counseling," *Journal of Religion and Health* 26, no. 4 (winter 1987): 309–22.

24. See Mary McGlone, "Healing the Spirit," *Holistic Nursing Practice* 4, no. 4 (July 1990): 78, 81.

25. See Suzanne C. Thompson and Jennifer Pitts, "Factors Relating to a Person's Ability to Find Meaning after a Diagnosis of Cancer," *Journal of Psychosocial Oncology* 11, no. 3 (1993): 1–21.

26. Wendy Schlessel Harpham has published three books; in addition to the two previously cited, *Diagnosis Cancer: Your Guide through the First Few Months* and *After Cancer: A Guide to Your New Life*, she has published *When a Parent Has Cancer: A Guide to Caring for Your Children* (New York: HarperCollins, 1997).

27. Reproductions of some of Tina Fletcher's paintings, along with artwork by other cancer survivors, are in a series of greeting cards called "Visions of Recovery," published by Zeneca Pharmaceutical Co. in coorperation with the Oncology Nursing Society, Wilmington, Del. 19850-5437.

28. LaTour, *Breast Cancer Companion*, 332. See also Ellen Carni's suggestion, in "Issues of Hope and Faith in the Cancer Patient," *Journal of Religion and Health* 27, no. 4 (winter 1988): 290, that cancer patients grappling with integrity and despair need to find creative pursuits that enrich their lives and make them feel inner-directed.

29. Mitchell L. Gaynor, *Healing Essence: A Cancer Doctor's Practical Program for Hope and Recovery* (New York: Kodansha International, 1995), 40, 223–24. In this book Gaynor, Assistant Clinical Professor of Medicine at the New York Hospital–Cornell Medical Center, describes the meditation program he uses in conjunction with conventional medical techniques.

30. Holland, "Cancer's Psychological Challenges," 161.

31. Francesca Morosani Thompson, *Going for the Cure* (New York: St. Martin's Press, 1989), 283–89.

Chapter 2.
How Do I See God Now? The Power of Sacred Images

1. See Andrew Lester's incisive discussion of the impact of God-images on the hoping process, in *Hope in Pastoral Care*, 82.

2. George Fitchett asserts the importance of spiritual assessment in directing our pastoral communication to central matters of belief and meaning, and our understanding of their implications for our actions. According to Fitchett, spiritual assessment includes the symbolic nature of religious objects and language. See *Assessing Spiritual Needs: A Guide for Caregivers* (Minneapolis: Augsburg, 1993), 20–45.

3. See Leroy Howe's provocative discussion of ambivalence in the representations of the image of God in the scriptures, in *The Image of God: A Theology for Pastoral Care and Counseling* (Nashville: Abingdon Press, 1995), 30, 87–88.

4. See James B. Ashbrook's discussion of the importance of searching for meaning in the cancer experience through metaphors and symbols, in "Living with Cancer," 79–83.

5. Lauren K. Ayers, *The Answer Is within You: Psychology, Women's Connections, and Breast Cancer* (New York: Crossroad, 1994), 38–39, 231–37. See the conclusions David Spiegel draws from research on relationships with women, in "Can Psychotherapy Prolong Cancer Survival? *Psychosomatics* 31, no. 4 (fall 1990): 364.

6. See Rosemary Radford Ruether's discussion in *Sexism and God-Talk: Toward a Feminist Theology* (Boston: Beacon Press, 1983), 23–24.

7. See Margaret L. Hammer's discussion of the value of maternal God-images in *Giving Birth: Reclaiming Biblical Metaphor for Pastoral Practice* (Louisville, Ky.: Westminster John Knox Press, 1994), 58, 204–9. See also Sallie McFague's comments on the power of maternal imagery of God, in *Models of God: Theology for an Ecological, Nuclear Age* (Philadelphia: Fortress Press, 1987), 113–66.

8. See my discussion of biblical images of God as Mother, in *In Whose Image? God and Gender* (New York: Crossroad, 1990), 21–26.

9. In "Competencies of the New (and Some Old) Spiritual Care Work," *Caregiver Journal* 12, no. 2 (1996): 4, Gordon J. Hilsman emphasizes the importance of pastoral caregivers not only knowing the content of a person's beliefs but also understanding how these beliefs contribute to that person's well-being.

10. See Sally McFague's discussion of the model of God as Friend in *Models of God*, 158–80.

11. Regina A. Coll, *Christianity and Feminism in Conversation* (Mystic, Conn.: Twenty-Third Publications, 1994), 45.

12. These pictures are by artist Doris Klein, of Fond du Lac, Wisconsin: Congregation of St. Agnes. Doris Klein's prints can be ordered through Heartbeats, 2259 Columbus Road, Cleveland, Ohio 44113.

13. According to Nelson Thayer, parental language about God tends to reinforce elements of personality left over from infantile psychosocial conflicts, and these unsatisfied dependency needs, feelings of conditional acceptance, and resentment of powerful parents subtly impede mature spirituality. See his discussion in *Spirituality and Pastoral Care* (Philadelphia: Fortress Press, 1985), 102–16.

14. Lester, *Hope in Pastoral Care*, 136.

Chapter 3.
Can I Still Hope? Sacred Stories That Bring Healing

1. See Thompson and Pitts, "Ability to Find Meaning after a Diagnosis of Cancer," 3.

2. Psychiatrist David Spiegel, in a landmark research study, discovered that women with metastatic breast cancer who received psychosocial intervention through supportive group therapy lived twice as long as those who did not receive this intervention. However, this study did not focus specifically on hope and its influence on survival. See David Spiegel, Joan R. Bloom, Helena C. Kraemer, and Ellen Gottheil, "Effects of Psychosocial Treatment on Survival

of Patients with Metastatic Breast Cancer," *Lancet* 2 (Oct. 14, 1989): 888–91. The Nowotny Hope Scale has been used to assess hope in women with breast cancer and to correlate hope with religiousness and spiritual well-being. See Mary Nowotny, "Assessment of Hope in Patients with Cancer: Development of an Instrument," *Oncology Nursing Forum* 16, no. 1 (January/February 1989): 57–61; Jacqueline Mickley, Karen Soeken, and Anne Belcher, "Spiritual Well-being, Religiousness and Hope among Women with Breast Cancer," *Image: Journal of Nursing Scholarship* 24, no. 4 (winter 1992): 267–72; Jacqueline Mickley and Karen Soeken, "Religiousness and Hope in Hispanic and Anglo-American Women with Breast Cancer," *Oncology Nursing Forum* 20, no. 8 (September 1993): 1171–77. The Nowotny Hope Scale holds potential for research studies to determine the relationship between hope and survival rate in people with cancer.

3. Post-White et al.,"Hope, Spirituality, Sense of Coherence," 1571.

4. Moltmann, *Theology of Hope*, 25.

5. Walter H. Capps, *The Future of Hope* (Philadelphia: Fortress Press, 1970), 28–30.

6. Emil L. Fackenheim, "The Commandment to Hope: A Response to Contemporary Jewish Experience," in Capps, *Future of Hope*, 68–69.

7. Lester, *Hope in Pastoral Care*, 36.

8. James Conlon, *Earth Story, Sacred Story* (Mystic, Conn.: Twenty-Third Publications, 1994), 10, 16, 19.

9. Ernest Kurtz and Katherine Ketcham, *The Spirituality of Imperfection: Modern Wisdom from Classic Stories* (New York: Bantam Books, 1992), 7–9.

10. Stanley Hauerwas and L. Gregory Jones, "Introduction: Why Narrative?" in *Why Narrative? Readings in Narrative Theology*, ed. Stanley Hauerwas and L. Gregory Jones (Grand Rapids: Wm. B. Eerdmans, Publishing Co., 1989), 1–2.

11. Martha Nussbaum, "Narrative Emotions: Beckett's Genealogy of Love," in Hauerwas and Jones, *Why Narrative? Readings in Narrative Theology*, 218, 225–29.

12. Johann Baptist Metz, "A Short Apology for Narrative," in Hauerwas and Jones, *Why Narrative? Readings in Narrative Theology*, 254–56.

13. Stephen Crites, "The Narrative Quality of Experience," *Journal of the American Academy of Religion* 39, no. 3 (September 1971): 291.

14. Ibid., 294–96.

15. Augustine, *Confessions*, trans. Henry Chadwick (New York: Oxford University Press, 1991), Book 11, chap. 20, p. 235.

16. Mark Jensen, "Life Histories and Narrative Theology," in *The Supervision of Pastoral Care*, ed. David A. Steere (Louisville, Ky.: Westminster John Knox Press, 1989), 114–15, 122–24.

17. Marvin W. Acklin, Earl C. Brown, and Paul A. Mauger, "The Role of Religious Values in Coping with Cancer," *Journal of Religion and Health* 22, no. 4 (winter 1983): 331.

18. Donald W. Musser, "On the Edge of Uncertainty: Twenty Years with Cancer," *Second Opinion* 5 (1987): 121–23.

19. In research with breast cancer patients, cognitive control through

construing benefit from the cancer experience was found to significantly predict adjustment. See Shelley E. Taylor, Rosemary R. Lichtman, and Joanne V. Wood, "Attributions, Beliefs about Control, and Adjustment to Breast Cancer," *Journal of Personality and Social Psychology* 46, no. 3 (March 1984): 489–502.

20. Shelley E. Taylor, "Adjustment to Threatening Events: A Theory of Cognitive Adaptation," *American Psychologist* 38, no. 11 (November 1983): 1161–65.

21. Crites, "Narrative Quality of Experience," 304.

22. Lester, *Hope in Pastoral Care*, 39.

23. See Charles V. Gerkin's *The Living Human Document: Re-Visioning Pastoral Counseling in a Hermeneutical Mode* (Nashville: Abingdon Press, 1984), 121–41, for an illustration of evoking stories in ways that open the possibility of reinterpretation and new direction.

24. Tim Eberhardt, "Storytelling and Pastoral Care," *Journal of Pastoral Care* 50, no. 1 (spring 1996): 27, 31.

Chapter 4.
What's Next? The Waiting Game

1. Musser, "On the Edge of Uncertainty," 125–26.

2. Glenna Halvorson-Boyd and Lisa K. Hunter, *Dancing in Limbo: Making Sense of Life after Cancer* (San Francisco: Jossey-Bass Publishers, 1995), 14. This book provides an excellent, clear description of emotional dynamics experienced by cancer survivors.

3. Harpham, *After Cancer*, 212–13.

4. Jennifer Hughes, *Cancer and Emotion* (New York: John Wiley & Sons, 1987), 54.

5. Harpham, *After Cancer*, 222.

6. Taylor, "Adjustment to Threatening Events," 1163, 1168–71.

7. E. Wayne Hill and Paul M. Mullen, "An Overview of Psychoneuroimmunology: Implications for Pastoral Care," *Journal of Pastoral Care* 50, no. 3 (fall 1996): 245. Hill and Mullen see the burgeoning field of psychoneuroimmunology as an unprecedented opportunity for the pastoral arts and sciences.

8. Larry Dossey, *Healing Words: The Power of Prayer and the Practice of Medicine* (San Francisco: HarperCollins, 1993), 205–6.

9. Hill and Mullen, "Overview of Psychoneuroimmunology," 245.

Chapter 5.
What Did I Do? Responsibility and Guilt

1. See Ayers, *Answer Is within You*, 52.

2. Fintel and McDermott, *Medical and Spiritual Guide*, 152–53.

3. Richard L. Schaper, "Pastoral Accompaniment of the Cancer Patient," *Journal of Religion and Health* 23, no. 2 (summer 1984): 143.

4. See also Halvorson-Boyd and Hunter, *Dancing in Limbo*, 44.

5. William Collinge, "Mind/Body Medicine: Separating the Hope from the Hype," *Coping* (winter 1992): 20.

6. Carni, "Issues of Hope and Faith," 286. See also David K. Wellisch and Joel Yager, "Is There a Cancer-Prone Personality?" *Cancer Journal for Clinicians* 33, no. 3 (May/June 1983): 145–51.

7. Richards and Palmer, "Cancer and Humiliation," 331–35.

8. See David Spiegel, "Can Psychotherapy Prolong Cancer Survival?" *Psychosomatics* 31, no. 4 (fall 1990): 363.

9. Richards and Palmer, "Cancer and Humiliation," 334.

10. Travis Maxwell and Jann Aldredge-Clanton, "Survivor Guilt in Cancer Patients: A Pastoral Perspective," *Journal of Pastoral Care* 48, no. 1 (spring 1994): 25–31.

11. Halvorson-Boyd and Hunter, *Dancing in Limbo*, 43–44.

12. Bonnie J. Miller-McLemore, "Death and the Moral Life: Odd Bedfellows in Our Postmodern Age," *Dialog* 32, no. 3 (summer 1993): 169.

13. *Cancer Facts and Figures—1996*, 10. Cigarette smoking is linked to 85 to 90 percent of all cases of lung cancer according to *Scientific American* 275, no. 3 (September 1996): 128.

14. See Michael E. Cavanagh, "Ministering to Cancer Patients," 233.

15. See Irene Henderson, "Matters Close to the Heart," in *Through the Eyes of Women: Insights for Pastoral Care*, ed. Jeanne Stevenson Moessner (Minneapolis: Fortress Press, 1996), 213.

16. Marie Fortune, *Sexual Violence, the Unmentionable Sin: An Ethical and Pastoral Perspective* (New York: Pilgrim Press, 1983), 209.

Chapter 6.
Where Do I Belong? The Social Consequences

1. Richards and Palmer, "Cancer and Humiliation," 333.

2. See Halvorson-Boyd and Hunter, *Dancing in Limbo*, 121–22.

3. See Hughes, *Cancer and Emotion*, 99–101.

4. See Clifford H. Swensen, Steffen Fuller, and Richard Clements, "Stage of Religious Faith and Reactions to Terminal Cancer," *Journal of Psychology and Theology* 21, no. 3 (fall 1993): 244.

5. See Barrie R. Cassileth, Edward J. Lusk, Thomas B. Strouse, David S. Miller, Lorraine Brown, and Patricia A. Cross, "A Psychological Analysis of Cancer Patients and Their Next-of-Kin," *Cancer* 55 (January 1985): 72–76, for a discussion of a research study demonstrating a mutuality of psychological response between patients and families, concluding that supportive intervention for the patient or relative who manifests distress should thus benefit both. See also David K. Wellisch, Deane L. Wolcott, Robert O. Pasnau, Fawzy I. Fawzy, and John Landsverk, "An Evaluation of the Psychosocial Problems of the Homebound Cancer Patient: Relationships of Patient Adjustment to Family Problems," *Journal of Psychosocial Oncology* 7, no. 1/2 (1989): 70–75, for a discussion of another research study that indicates the importance of family assessment and intervention skills in working with homebound cancer patients.

6. Lester, *Hope in Pastoral Care*, 98–99.

7. Spiegel et al., "Effects of Psychosocial Treatment," 888–91; Spiegel, "Can Psychotherapy Prolong Cancer Survival?" 361–65.

8. Ayers, *Answer Is within You*, 56, 232.

9. David K. Wellisch, "Beyond the Year 2000: The Future of Groups for Patients with Cancer," *Cancer Practice* 1, no. 3 (September/October 1993): 198.

10. Henderson, "Matters Close to the Heart," 220.

11. Swensen, Fuller, and Clements, "Stage of Religious Faith," 242, 245.

12. Larry Dossey, "What's Love Got to Do with It?" *Alternative Therapies* 2, no. 3 (May 1996): 13–14.

Chapter 7.
Who Am I Now? Embodiment and Sexuality

1. Johnson and Klein, *I Can Cope*, 120–36.

2. Cavanagh, "Ministering to Cancer Patients," 234.

3. See Barbara Rubin Wainrib and Sandra Haber, with Jack Maguire, *Prostate Cancer: A Guide for Women and the Men They Love* (New York: Doubleday, 1996), 219–41.

4. Ellen R. Gritz, David K. Wellisch, He-Jing Wang, Jessie Siau, John A. Landsverk, and Malcolm D. Cosgrove, "Long-Term Effects of Testicular Cancer on Sexual Functioning in Married Couples," *Cancer* 4, no. 7 (October 1989): 1563–67.

5. Johnson and Klein, *I Can Cope*, 121–23.

6. Wendy S. Schain, David K. Wellisch, Robert O. Pasnau, and John Landsverk, "The Sooner the Better: A Study of Psychological Factors in Women Undergoing Immediate versus Delayed Breast Reconstruction," *American Journal of Psychiatry* 142, no. 1 (January 1985): 45–46.

7. Hughes, *Cancer and Emotion*, 56.

8. Wainrib and Haber, *Prostate Cancer*, 241–42.

9. See Nessim and Ellis, *Cancervive*, 220–48.

10. McFague, *Models of God*, 146–47.

11. Nouwen, *Wounded Healer*, 95.

12. Matthew Fox, *The Coming of the Cosmic Christ* (San Francisco: Harper & Row, 1988), 3, 144–51.

13. See Howard Clinebell, *Ecotherapy: Healing Ourselves, Healing the Earth* (New York: Haworth Press, 1996), 1–15, 188–232.

14. Doris Klein, "The Torn Woman"; see chap. 2, n. 12.

Chapter 8.
What Treatment Should I Choose? The Ethical Dilemma

1. Quoted in Wainrib and Haber, *Prostate Cancer*, 129–30.

2. Ibid., 146–52.

3. See David K. Wellisch, Robin DiMatteo, Melvin Silverstein, John Landsverk, Robert Hoffman, James Waisman, Neal Handel, Ellen Waisman-Smith, and Wendy Schain, "Psychosocial Outcomes of Breast Cancer Thera-

pies: Lumpectomy versus Mastectomy," *Psychosomatics* 30, no. 4 (fall 1989): 365–73. The lumpectomy patients in this study had a more intact body image and a greater sense of sexual desirability than those who had mastectomy with breast reconstruction and those who had mastectomy without breast reconstruction.

4. See Howard P. Greenwald, *Who Survives Cancer?* (Berkeley: University of California Press, 1992), 37–46.

5. Lloyd J. Old, "Immunotherapy for Cancer," *Scientific American* 275, no. 3 (September 1996): 136–43.

6. Allen Oliff, Jackson B. Gibbs, and Frank McCormick, "New Molecular Targets for Cancer Therapy," *Scientific American* 275, no. 3 (September 1996): 144–49.

7. Barrie R. Cassileth, Edward J. Lusk, Thomas B. Strouse, and Brenda Bodenheimer, "Contemporary Unorthodox Treatments in Cancer Medicine," *Annals of Internal Medicine* 101, no. 1 (1984): 111–12.

8. Jean-Jacques Aulas, "Alternative Cancer Treatments," *Scientific American* 275, no. 3 (September 1996): 162–63.

9. See J. Vincent Guss, Jr., "Guidelines Detail the Chaplain's Role in Bioethics Consultation," *Medical Ethics Advisor* 9, no. 5 (May 1993): 61–63.

10. See Judith Caron's discussion of ethical vision and values in *Christian Ethics: Shaping Values, Vision, Decisions* (Mystic, Conn.: Twenty-Third Publications, 1995), 36–48, 84–93.

11. See interpretations of beneficence and autonomy in Glenn C. Graber and David C. Thomasma, *Theory and Practice in Medical Ethics* (New York: Continuum, 1989), 30–35, 59–61.

12. Eric J. Cassell, "Recognizing Suffering," *Hastings Center Report* (May/June 1991): 26.

13. Caron, *Christian Ethics*, 221–22.

14. Ibid., 230.

15. See Martina Darrah and Pat Milmoe McCarrick, "Managed Health Care: New Ethical Issues for All," *Kennedy Institute of Ethics Journal* 6, no. 2 (June 1996): 189–92; Ezekiel J. Emanuel, "Medical Ethics in the Era of Managed Care: The Need for Institutional Structures Instead of Principles for Individual Cases," *Journal of Clinical Ethics* 6, no. 4 (winter 1995): 335–36; David Orentlicher, "Physician Advocacy for Patients under Managed Care," *Journal of Clinical Ethics* 6, no. 4 (winter 1995): 333–34; Laurie Zoloth-Dorfman and Susan Rubin, "The Patient as Commodity: Managed Care and the Question of Ethics," *Journal of Clinical Ethics* 6, no. 4 (winter 1995): 339–57.

16. Greenwald, *Who Survives Cancer?* 5–19.

Chapter 9.
How Much Time Do I Have? The Many Faces of Hope and Healing

1. J. William Worden, "The Experience of Recurrent Cancer," *Cancer Journal for Clinicians* 39, no. 5 (September/October 1989): 309–10; Weisman and Worden, " Emotional Impact of Recurrent Cancer," 8–10.

2. Schaper, "Pastoral Accompaniment of the Cancer Patient," 145–46.

3. Cantor, *And a Time to Live,* 223.

4. Cassell, "Recognizing Suffering," 24–25.

5. Post-White et al., "Hope, Spirituality, Sense of Coherence," 1575–76.

6. Gaynor, *Healing Essence,* 222–23.

7. Fintel and McDermott, *Medical and Spiritual Guide,* 216.

8. John Carmody, *Cancer and Faith: Reflections on Living with a Terminal Illness* (Mystic, Conn.: Twenty-Third Publications, 1994), 12–13, 90–91, 131, 137–38.

9. Bonnie J. Miller-McLemore emphasizes the importance of rituals in helping people to reconsider their lives, to make amends, and to reclaim their beliefs. See "Death and the Moral Life," 170. See also Carni, "Issues of Hope and Faith," 287.

10. Doris Klein, "The Midwives"; see chap. 2, n. 12.

11. I am grateful to Peggy for her permission to include these quotations from her journal.

Index